Cheyenne
Bottoms

Cheyenne Bottoms

WETLAND IN JEOPARDY

John L. Zimmerman

 University Press of Kansas

Color photographs following page 110 courtesy of Kansas Department of Wildlife and Parks. Photographs of white-faced ibis and green-winged teal are by
Gene Brehm; all others are by Mike Blair.

Published by the University Press of Kansas (Lawrence, Kansas 66045), which
was organized by the Kansas Board of Regents and is operated and funded by
Emporia State University, Fort Hays State University, Kansas State University,
Pittsburg State University, the University of Kansas, and Wichita State University

Library of Congress Cataloging in Publication Data

Zimmerman, John L., 1933–
    Cheyenne Bottoms, wetland in jeopardy / John L. Zimmerman.
      p. cm.
    Includes bibliographical references and index.
    ISBN 0-7006-0443-X (alk. paper)
    1. Habitat (Ecology)—Kansas—Cheyenne Bottoms.   2. Natural history—
Kansas—Cheyenne Bottoms.   3. Cheyenne Bottoms (Kan.) 4. Wetland ecology—Kansas—Cheyenne Bottoms.   I. Title.
QH105.K3Z56   1990
574.5′26325′0978152—dc20   90-12907
                                                            CIP

British Library Cataloging in Publication Data is available.

Printed in the United States of America
10 9 8 7 6 5 4 3 2 1

When the history of the Environmental Revolution is written, perhaps the effort to save Cheyenne Bottoms will be briefly mentioned. But these few lines will testify to the power of hope, vision, and determination of many good folks. It is to these people that this book is dedicated.

And to Taylor Renée and her generation, with hope for an Earth still rich in the diversity with which it has been naturally endowed.

Contents

List of Illustrations

LIST OF ILLUSTRATIONS

Foreword

"Here I stand. I can do no other. God help me. Amen."
—Martin Luther, 1521

In the fall of 1983 something important happened in Kansas. Like the ripples from a tiny pebble tossed into a quiet pool, the effects of that event still radiate outward, far from the source. Maybe all big changes start small. This one surely did. Five people made a trip to Cheyenne Bottoms one hot September day in 1983 to find out from Stan Wood, the current refuge manager, whether the rumors were true. Was Cheyenne Bottoms really drying up? The answer: yes, it was.

Others had walked away at that news, sadly shaking their heads at the enormity of the coming loss. But here was a watershed moment; these five refused to acquiesce. Rather than yielding in silent submission, they resolved, like Luther at Worms, to plant their feet and say, "Here we stand." That was the pebble.

The word spread that Cheyenne Bottoms was in trouble and needed help. Help came in abundance. All of Kansas' major conservation organizations joined together in a crusade—Kansas Audubon Council, Ducks Unlimited, Kansas Wildlife Federation, the Wildlife Society, Sierra Club, Kansas Natural Resource Council, American Fisheries Society, Kansas Ornithological Society. Many of these groups had never communicated with each other before; many were downright suspicious of each other.

But all agreed that Cheyenne Bottoms should be saved and that they would work together to do it.

The ripples spread. Garden clubs and sportsmen's clubs, grade school and high school classes, Audubon and Sierra units, the Kansas Rural Center, national environmental and wildlife organizations, all joined in support of the Bottoms. Best of all, lots and lots of "just plain folks" said over and over again that Cheyenne Bottoms had been a part of their childhood, an experience in their coming of age. They didn't want to see it die. Hundreds, perhaps thousands, of people spoke out.

First they simply wrote letters. Soon a task force was organized to instigate a legislative study of the water and engineering needs of the Bottoms. To promote this bill ordinary people indicated their sponsorship by purchasing "Save the Bottoms" seat cushions that were delivered to each legislator. With each cushion came this pitch: We're taking care of your bottoms; please take care of ours! Members and friends of the Kansas Chapter of the Wildlife Society ran a vial of Bottoms water from Great Bend to the Capitol and presented each lawmaker with a little brown jug of genuine Cheyenne Bottoms water, some very precious stuff. Posters, brochures, bumper stickers, and T-shirts advertised the plight of the wetlands.

The message from these Kansans rang through the legislature. In 1985, not only did the legislators authorize funding for a study of the problems at Cheyenne Bottoms, they also agreed to pay for part of the study with general revenue funds. Never before in Kansas history had taxpayers' dollars gone toward wildlife needs. The ripples were widening.

Today Cheyenne Bottoms has achieved worldwide recognition for its value to migratory shorebirds. This book will tell that story and more. But Cheyenne Bottoms is not out of danger. The state-sanctioned death of the Arkansas

River and the increased development of water resources in the area surrounding the Bottoms continue to bleed the Bottoms' annual rights to 50,000 acre-feet of water. Management is hampered by liability for flood damage on adjacent properties during times of abundant water, dense cattail stands, high evaporation rates, and a host of other problems. More than two years after the completion of the hard-won feasibility study, restoration plans are still evolving. The need for voices expressing their concern for Cheyenne Bottoms is as strong as ever.

Many times over the course of the efforts to save Cheyenne Bottoms, we were told that we didn't have a chance, that the forces of opposition and the power of tradition were too strong. If we had heard only with our ears and not with our hearts, the battle to save the Bottoms would have ended long ago. But we carried with us a vision, fired by the belief that together we could turn the tide of opinion, that we could make others see what we saw, and that we could teach them to value wetlands and wildlife. We refused to surrender to doubt and to doubters.

There is a lesson here that we must remember as we look beyond Cheyenne Bottoms toward our environmental future. The power of choice is ours. If we exercise it, we may yet save our planet. We must again and again plant our feet and say, "Here we stand. We will lose no more wildlife. We will lose no more wetlands. We will not let the Earth die."

It is appropriate that John Zimmerman is writing this story now. John first introduced me to the concept of Spaceship Earth and taught me the word "ecology." He took me on my first trip to Cheyenne Bottoms. Without his influence, I would not be doing what I am doing today. Thanks, John.

Manhattan, Kansas   Jan Garton

Acknowledgments

My enthusiasm for Cheyenne Bottoms has been renewed annually by the contagious awe and wonder of the hundreds of students who have joined me on excursions to the Bottoms over the past quarter century. My special thanks, however, go to Marvin Schwilling and Ed Martinez, who have taught me out of their intimate knowledge of the marsh. This book would not have been possible without the data base provided by the assessment study conducted by the Kansas Biological and Geological Surveys. I sincerely thank these scientists for this important work. But their study could never have been carried out without the funding provided by the Kansas Legislature, which in turn would never have authorized the expenditure without the overwhelming concern for the Bottoms expressed by the people of Kansas. Hence, it is to Jan Garton and the citizens who desired to save the Bottoms that I owe the greatest debt of gratitude.

The idea that the assessment study could be converted into a less technical book originated with the staff of the University Press of Kansas. I thank them for the opportunity to try my mind at this and for their instrumental role in the transformation of this idea and my efforts into the reality you now hold.

The effectiveness of this book has been immeasurably increased by Martin B. Capron's drawings. His interpretive skill and especially his sensitivity to nature have been a joy to me, as I think it will be for you as well. Thanks, Marty.

I appreciate the support of W. Alan Wentz, assistant secretary, Department of Wildlife and Parks, and his staff for their efforts in making information available and apprising me of the state of the management plan being developed under the able direction of Laurie Yasui. Special thanks are due as well to Mike Blair and Gene Brehm for their outstanding photographic work.

A number of people have contributed information and thoughts to the development of my ideas about the Bottoms. While I assume responsibility for the opinions expressed in this book, I especially acknowledge my debt to Gary Hulett of Governor Hayden's staff, Jan Garton, and Bob Kruh and Spencer Tomb of Kansas State University. Permission to cite unpublished materials has been given by Brian A. Harrington of the Manomet Bird Observatory and Gonzalo Castro and Fritz Knopf at Colorado State University. I owe special thanks to Lou Ann Claassen of the Division of Biology at Kansas State for assistance in manuscript preparation.

Cheyenne
Bottoms

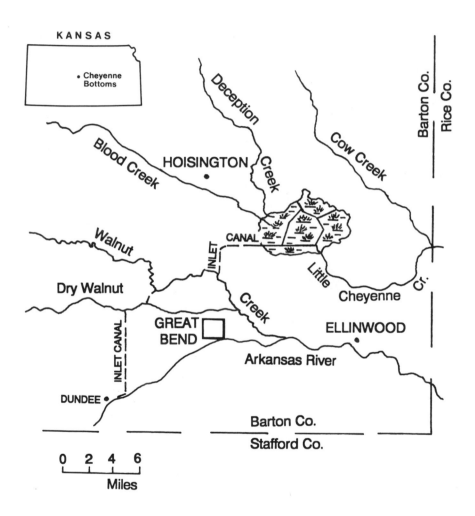

KANSAS

• Cheyenne
  Bottoms

Deception Creek

Blood Creek

HOISINGTON

Cow Creek

Barton Co.

Rice Co.

Walnut

CANAL

INLET

Little Cheyenne Cr.

Dry Walnut

Creek

INLET CANAL

GREAT BEND

ELLINWOOD

Arkansas River

DUNDEE

Barton Co.

Stafford Co.

0 2 4 6

Miles

1 "An Insuperable Obstacle"

The periodic sheets of ice that characterized the Pleistocene immobilized so much water that ocean levels were 300 feet lower than they are today. Humans, aggressively probing their horizons, crossed dry-shod from Asia through Beringea during this glacial epoch and moved southward into North America along ice-free corridors. Sometime during the last glacial advance they entered the central Great Plains; they left no record of their initial impressions, but the debris scattered in the wake of their passing generations gives evidence that they lived on the land for thousands and thousands of years, prospering when times were good, suffering when times were bad.

Written history arrived with the first Europeans under the command of Don Francisco Vásquez de Coronado in 1541. They came with both the predisposition and the paraphernalia to record their experiences. Coronado crossed the Arkansas River at what is now Ford, Kansas, traveled downstream for about four days, left the river at the great bend to pass through the area we now know as Cheyenne Bottoms, and continued on to the Land of Quivira in present-day Rice County, Kansas. Juan Jaramillo, a horseman in Coronado's *entrada*, described the region to "be very fruitful in all sorts of products." Coronado reported that "the country itself is the best I have ever seen for producing all the products of Spain, . . . the land itself being very flat and black and being very well watered by the rivulets and springs and rivers."

Lt. Zebulon Pike arrived at the Arkansas River at the mouth of Walnut Creek near present-day Great Bend, Kansas, in mid-October 1806. He noted that although the valley of the Arkansas was nearly 500 yards wide from bank to bank, the water was only 6 inches deep and the stream was no more than 20 feet wide. The party lingered for nine days on the south bank of the river, and after building two canoes, six members of the party led by Lt. James Wilkinson returned east on October 28 by floating downstream—at least when they could. Sometimes the water was too shallow, and that particular year, at times the river was full of ice. Pike continued west to the head-waters of the Arkansas and an eventual confrontation with the descendants of the Spanish colonists who came after Coronado. Cheyenne Bottoms must have impressed Pike, since he referred to it again in his summary as a "low and swampy" area within 15 or 20 miles of the river and covered with "ponds extending out from the [north bank of the] river." Perhaps Pike's view of the wetlands resulted from his contrasting general impression of the region as a water-starved land, useless for farming—"a barren soil, parched and dried up for eight months in the year"; it would be best to "leave the prairies incapable of cultiva-tion to the wandering and uncivilized aborigines of the country." This conclusion was reinforced by the Stephen H. Long expedition. During the late summer of 1820 a contingent under Captain J. R. Bell separated from the main party and returned to Fort Smith from Colorado by coming down the Arkansas River and stopped for a day at the mouth of Walnut Creek to allow their horses to take advantage of the good forage. The account of this journey described the region of the Arkansas drainage as "wholly unfit for cultivation, and of course, uninhabitable by a

people depending upon agriculture for their subsistence
. . . the scarcity of wood and water, almost uniformly
prevalent, will prove an insuperable obstacle in the way of
settling the country." It was Long who identified this region on the map as "The Great American Desert."

The contrast between Coronado's account and that of
the American explorers about two hundred fifty years
later is not an indication of climatic change. In fact, evidence suggests that the years of Pike's and Long's expeditions were wetter than the period of Coronado's incursion
into the plains. The difference was a matter of perspective
and frame of reference. To eastern North Americans, trees
signified good soil and productivity, while grasslands de-
noted sterility. To the Spanish, on the other hand, the lush
mixed-grass prairies punctuated with patches of wildflowers and seeping springs indicated fertility, in contrast to
the true deserts of Chihuahua and Sonora. Yet the idea of
a desert stretching beyond the Missouri to the base of the
western mountains persisted. In the late 1850s, Lt. G. K.
Warren, on still another government survey, concluded
that the ninety-seventh meridian was the limit of ordinary
agriculture. And if one assumes that "ordinary" refers to
agriculture dependent upon rainfall, that is, the agriculture of the Midwest and the East, he was quite correct. For
to the west of this general longitude the amount of moisture lost to evaporation from the surface of the land and
the vegetation growing on it (evapotranspiration) exceeds
that received from rainfall. It is a land of water deficit.

After the Civil War, the cattle drives north from Texas
began in earnest as the railroads pushed west, the first
cattle being shipped from Abilene in 1867 and from Ells-
worth, about 30 miles northeast of Cheyenne Bottoms,
five years later. After the economic panic of 1873, cattle
drives became less frequent; and with the drought that
began at the end of the century, the open range was re-

placed by ranches and farmsteads as people sequestered the water necessary for existence with barriers of recently invented barbed wire.

The Federal Homestead Act had already been passed in 1862, and its implementation was encouraged by the railroads and by land speculators, who replaced the notion of the Great American Desert with what Henry Nash Smith called the "myth of the garden." Josiah Gregg predicted as early as 1844 that cultivation would ameliorate the dry climate. F. V. Hayden, director of the U.S. Geological Surveys of the Territories, suggested in 1867 that trees planted on the prairie would contribute moisture to the atmosphere. Dr. Samuel Aughey of Nebraska argued that cultivation not only increases the absorption of water into the soil, but the increase in humidity caused by the cycle of evaporation from soil and crops and the deposition of dew would increase rainfall. Charles Dana Wilber, a land speculator and amateur scientist, compressed this speculation into a slogan, "rain follows the plow," that soon became the prime faith-statement undergirding the struggle for self-sufficiency and ultimate affluence for settlers throughout the Great Plains.

Beginning in 1865 and during the boom years of the early 1880s, rainfall actually was increasing. During 1877 in Dodge City, for example, rainfall was about 50 percent greater than the average for the region. And the population increased along with the moisture. In 1885 the population density of Sherman County, on the High Plains of Kansas, was one person per 10 square miles, increasing by a factor of thirty within just the next year to three people per square mile and again doubling in density by 1889. The entire population of southwestern Kansas increased twenty-fold during the decade of the 1880s. A Dodge City reporter stated at the height of the boom that western Kansans no longer feared the desert. But the euphoria of hope was replaced with the reality of drought, and settlers returned east during the last decade of the nineteenth century with "In God we trusted, in Kansas we busted" scrawled across the canopies of their wagons. Or as Walter Prescott Webb related, " 'This,' said the newcomer to the Plains, 'would be a fine country if we just had water.' 'Yes,' answered the man whose wagon tongue pointed east, 'so would hell.' " Western Kansas lost half its population between 1888 and 1892. A Kansas jurist named Kinney wrote that "the only crop that has grown surely and abundantly year in and year out in that territory . . . is the crop of despair."

If rainfall from the sky was finally recognized as insufficient, then perhaps surface water flow in rivers could be used to irrigate the land and provide reliability for the production of crops. Water was there for the using; in 1872 there was enough water coming down the Arkansas River to float thousands of railroad ties all the way from Colorado to Great Bend. A canal company was organized in Finney County in 1880 to use the water of the Arkansas, and by the end of the decade more than 400 miles of canals and ditches had been constructed in the Garden City area. Clark E. Carr, an investor in the Garden City irrigation projects, contended that "the valleys and basins of the Rocky mountains have been converted into a vast watering pot . . . the Arkansas river is the spout, and the artificial ditches men have made, the perforated nozzle." Canals were completed also at Lakin, Dodge City, Kinsley, and Larned. The water was there, and the hope of prosperity for every town along the river demanded that this free resource be channeled for productive uses. But in the summer of 1896, the Arkansas River was completely dry at Garden City, partly because of drought but certainly because of widespread diversion, not only in Kansas but also upstream in Colorado. By the end of the nineteenth cen-

An abandoned windmill testifies to the continual struggle for a sustainable livelihood in the Great American Desert.

tury, nobody believed that surface waters were adequate to meet the demands of agriculture. The failure of river diversion ultimately led to the federal Newlands Reclamation Act of 1902, but as a result of its topography, Kansas was left out during the early days of the big dam business.

Kansans had to find another method to provide water for agriculture. Kansas Sen. John J. Ingalls described windmills as "vivacious disks disturb[ing] the monotony of the sky." The technology of tapping groundwater with wind-driven pumps was satisfactory for the cattle industry and was already in use across Kansas. But the immense volume of water required by crop agriculture could not be sustained even by the seemingly perpetual Kansas wind. Needs drive innovations, however. Improvements in technology resulted in better pumps powered by electricity and natural gas and eventually allowed the sinking of wells into the Ogallala, Cheyenne, and Dakota aquifers. In 1904 the Ogallala was considered to be a gigantic underground river flowing forever from the western mountains to the sea.

Irrigation with groundwater rapidly expanded between 1940 and 1960 as a result of war-generated demand, increased markets, and governmental support for agricultural products, although by 1960 nobody believed in the myth of an inexhaustible supply of underground water. Center pivot irrigation, first introduced in the 1950s, became common in the 1970s. A count from satellite telemetry of the infrared fingerprints of the 135-acre circles produced by center pivot systems showed an increase in the Great Plains from fewer than 3,000 in 1972 to over 17,000 by 1978! The withdrawal of water from the Ogallala increased by 300 percent from 1950 to 1980 to a rate that was over ten times the recharge rate. Fossil water was being mined; the resource had become nonrenewable in a historic time scale. John Janovy, an ecologist at the University of Nebraska, compared the packed circles of center pivots as seen from the air to electronmicrographs of virus particles within an infected cell, sucking out the very lifeblood of the prairie. Between 1973 and 1985 the water table declined on an average of 3 feet per year in southwestern Kansas, and by the early 1980s, on average, 30 percent of the water saturating the strata of the Ogallala aquifer had been removed. It has been estimated that, once depleted, it will take 7,000 years to recharge the Ogallala aquifer in Kansas. But that prediction antedated the realization that the greenhouse effect is producing global warming, which will probably result in decreased rainfall in the Great Plains. In truth, the Ogallala may never be recharged.

In colonial times, the townspeople used the village green, the commons, for the grazing of cattle. As Garrett Hardin emphasized over twenty years ago, such a system was bound to fail since each livestock owner, of necessity, had to increase his use of the commons to maximize his own gain, ultimately leading to the presence of too many cattle on too little grass and ultimate destruction of the common resource. The "tragedy of the commons" was repeated in western Kansas through the overgrazing of the open range in the 1880s and the exploitation of surface waters by diversion ditches in the 1890s. And current demand continues to deplete fossil groundwaters in the present decade. As late as 1964 James E. Taylor would write that "those who have studied the water problem in Kansas indicate that an *adequate supply should be provided for the beneficial use by all* [italics mine] . . . it is believed that the present state agency can obtain these ends, if it will, by wise and proper administration." Such a naive disregard for the reality of the tragedy of the commons led Morton Bittinger and Elizabeth Green to conclude in 1980 that "the effectiveness of local ground-water management districts in stopping depletion is essentially nil." A Garden City farmer commented with understanding insight that "I've always known that it's foolish to pump that water out, but economics has forced me to do it." Craig Miner writes that there is a lesson to be learned from the experiences of settling western Kansas in the century past: "Humankind cannot limitlessly manipulate physical environments and . . . when traditional ideas of the civilizing process are applied to an environment with obvious and

Aerial view of center pivots, pockmarks of the tragedy of the commons.

immediate limits, success itself, as defined by the civilizing culture, breeds ultimate failure." The lesson, unfortunately, has not been learned, even though many believe that the truth and its consequences will be manifest before the beginning of the next century.

Studies by David Kromm and Stephen White have shown that over three-fourths of the people in southwestern Kansas realize that their economy and well-being are dependent upon changes in groundwater. Although irrigators and those employed in agribusiness have the least concern over groundwater depletion, their ranking of this problem below other concerns, like the cost of fuel, simply reflects the realities of doing business, not a lack of awareness of the relentless reduction of the natural capital upon which their business depends. Indeed, irrigators are sensitive to resource depletion and have attempted to mitigate the rate of loss by switching to crops that demand less water, conservation tillage, tailwater reuse, and improved methods of irrigation. And the rate of decline in the water table actually had decreased for a period beginning in 1980 but then increased again to a decline of 3 feet per year during the drought of 1988. As with the other schemes of environmental exploitation that preceded it on the High Plains, the use of groundwater for irrigation will end also. Donald Green predicts, "Gradually, farmer after farmer will simply find it uneconomical to spend more money in order to get less water from the ground." The return to nonirrigated agriculture is already happening in the southern High Plains. As one Kansas ecologist recently commented, "If you want to predict the future of western Kansas, visit Lubbock."

Perhaps Pike was correct. Maybe we should not have come, but we're here. We have developed a technological society in a land where water is deficient, and any contemporary understanding of Cheyenne Bottoms must consider an environmental matrix that takes this into account. At this moment in the history of the Great Plains, the ecological patterns and processes that I describe in the following chapters are not only dependent upon the topography and soil, the biota, and the climatic vagaries of the region, but are also intermingled with, indeed, shackled to, humankind's attempts to manage lives and enterprises from an antagonistic posture in a continuing confrontation with the Great American Desert, perhaps "an insuperable obstacle" after all. Cheyenne Bottoms has had a long past. If the Bottoms is to have a future, a future that will continue to permit its essential contribution as a life-support system for increasingly scarce wetland plants and animals as well as a significant proportion of hemispheric wildlife populations, then decisions must be made and conservation strategies implemented. But there is a cost; and if long-term solutions are truly sought, the cost will involve considerable sacrifice by all of us in the ways we live and strive for material well-being. Not to decide, however, is also a decision; then the sacrifice will be even greater be-

Ghost of the Ark

cause it will be one of the spirit rather than of mere things. Our life will become more grindingly cruel, not only because of the irrevocable decrease in the diversity of life on this planet but also because of our disregard for the admonitions of the Sixth Day to be the stewards of the Earth's grand bounty.

2　The Basin

Unexpected changes in terrain are certainly impressive. How many of us recall parking the car at Desert View for the first time, walking a few yards in utter innocence, and then being overwhelmed by the initial sight of the Grand Canyon falling away at our feet? Even in the Great Plains, comparable experiences can occur. I can remember flying low across the Llano Estacado on the night of a winter full moon, the dense air utterly transparent, the landscape all chiaroscuro, and being startled by the ground's descent into the slash of Palo Duro Canyon under the nose of the aircraft. The basin of Cheyenne Bottoms is not that dramatic. As with just about everything in Kansas except the weather, the contrast in the terrain is subtle. The effect is more subliminal than conscious. It is dependent upon the reality of what has gone before, upon context.

While I may not like the tone of Merrill Gilfillan's angry condemnation of man's devastation of the Arkansas River valley, the description is valid: "Wheat jammed in to the very banks, leaving not a single tree for 20 miles along one of the continent's major rivers. It is a fouled mess and monotone, an ignoble extreme of the slash and burn." But to come to the edge of the basin and see the blues and greens of Cheyenne Bottoms spread out below, the flocks of pelicans wheeling in the thermals, flashing white and then disappearing as they turn in the sun, presents an abrupt and most welcome change of scene.

You and I would not be the first to be so affected. On Wednesday, October 15, 1806, Zebulon Montgomery Pike, Lieutenant, U.S. Army, after traveling south from the Republican River and fording the Smoky Hill about 6 miles northwest of what is now Dorrance, crossed over the divide between the Smoky Hill and Arkansas River drainages and entered a basin, a low prairie "nearly all covered with ponds." The army medical doctor and early ornithologist Elliott Coues identified this site as Cheyenne Bottoms in his 1895 account of Pike's expedition. Even in those pristine days, when prairie wetlands were cast abundantly across the landscape in scattered seeps and depressions, the Bottoms appeared worthy of note. This elliptical depression is small, only about 64 square miles in area, and is bounded on the north, south, and west by terraced bluffs, their tops rising about 100 feet above the basin floor. This subtle escarpment is composed of sediments laid down about 100 million years ago during the Cretaceous period. The eastern and southeastern sides of the basin are formed by lower ridges of dune sand and silt, deposited there by wind and water during the late Pleistocene, almost just yesterday.

A much longer time ago, when the first evidence of life was preserved in the primordial oceans, the area of Cheyenne Bottoms was a sterile, lifeless landscape of isolated hills that rose several hundred feet above the lowlands. Five hundred million years ago, an extended period of intermittent flooding and regression by shallow seas—teeming with a diversity of life that represented all the major groups of animals and most of the plants—began and continued until the end of the Paleozoic. Then about 250 million years ago, the land again emerged as the sea withdrew. For about 100 million years the terrain apparently remained above water, but there are no strata representative of this period in the rocks underneath Cheyenne Bottoms.

In the early Cretaceous, arms of the sea encroached from both the north and the south to inundate the region once again. The record in the rocks reveals that during this period Cheyenne Bottoms was alternately covered by the brackish backwaters of marine embayments or buried in the sediments from rivers whose velocities were reduced in the dendritic patterns of deltas flowing into these Cretaceous seas. Turtles and crocodiles occurred in these shallows, and the first true land plants, the evergreen conifers, grew in the uplands where early mammals scampered among their trunks. The seas were dominated by aquatic carnivores, reptiles like paddle-footed mosasaurs and plesiosaurs and the more ancient sharks, which fed on a great variety of bony fish. Some of these fish inhabited reeflike communities that developed in association with giant clams, whose lightweight shells were as large as four feet in diameter. Unlike modern clams, they lay on their sides on top of the fine silt that covered the sea bottom, providing a substrate for oysters, barnacles, and tube-dwelling worms. Species of coiled cephalopods related to the contemporary chambered nautilus were present in great diversity. Giant squids moved by jet propulsion through these productive waters in search of their invertebrate prey.

Overhead the pterosaurs soared and flapped. These flying reptiles shared the airspace with a diversity of birds, an assemblage that probably had some similarity to that which can be seen there today. Although there are no fossil data from the Bottoms, the late Cretaceous avifauna elsewhere probably included grebes, loons, cormorants, ibis, various shorebirds, and rails. There were some strangers too, as demonstrated by the Niobrara deposits of the

Predators flourished in the seas that covered Cheyenne Bottoms during the Cretaceous. Squid, nautili, and sharks move through the depths in search of prey. A plesiosaur snares a squid; the flightless, toothed Hesperornis *gathers morsels from the feast, unaware of the approach of*

*the giant mosasaur that dominated these ancient seas. Overhead a Pter-
anodon passes, perhaps to catch a small fish driven to the surface by a
pursuing* Hesperornis.

late Cretaceous. This was the time of the toothed birds, the ternlike *Ichthyornis* and the loonlike *Hesperornis* that was derived from flying ancestors but had already evolved into flightlessness. Both birds were first known to scientists in the 1870s from Kansas deposits.

About 60 or 70 million years ago, during the late Cretaceous, the uplift associated with the initial development of the Rocky Mountains began and the oceans withdrew from the central plains for the last time. The dinosaurs disappeared. *Ichthyornis* and *Hesperornis* also became extinct during this period, but other bird species lived on, leaving descendants that still can be found in the region. Sometime between the late Cretaceous, 100 million years ago, and the early Pliocene, just 5 million years ago, tectonic movements in underlying rock strata deep within the mantle of the planet occurred, dropping the surface of the Earth to form the basin of Cheyenne Bottoms. About 10 million years ago in the middle Miocene the Front Range began its uplift, giving to the region of Cheyenne Bottoms its rainshadow of semiaridity that would affect all life, including humankind's, in the years to come.

The newly formed Rocky Mountains eroded as they rose during the late Miocene, contributing a wide apron of gravel, sand, and silt that was carried east across the plains by wind and water during the Pliocene, decreasing in thickness with increasing distance from the mountains of its origin. Much of this deposition has since been carried into the sea, but what remains is now known as the Ogallala Formation, a repository of fossil water upon which the economy of the High Plains depends and the hopes of management plans for Cheyenne Bottoms once relied. Life in the basin of Cheyenne Bottoms during the late Miocene was both familiar and strange. The inconspicuous mammals of the Cretaceous evergreen forests had now become dominant, populating the savannalike plains with rhinoceros, horses, camels, saber-toothed cats, and peccaries. Sunfish, crayfish, and bullfrogs lived in the streams, which were bordered by cottonwoods, mulberry, willows, elms, and hackberry. Almost all the modern families of birds would be recognized in both terrestrial and aquatic habitats. Grasses that would later come to dominate the region appeared for the first time.

The drying winds of the prevailing westerlies blowing down from the Rocky Mountains—deprived of moisture in the passage over the Continental Divide and heated by the descent to the plains—converted the more mesic savannas of the Miocene into open prairies of grass by the beginning of the Pleistocene, about 2 million years ago. A stream flowed across the exposed Cretaceous rocks in the basin of Cheyenne Bottoms, carrying water that was part of the Smoky Hill drainage, which in those days flowed south into the Arkansas River. The dry winds also carried soil, producing a prolonged dust bowl of unknown proportions. But enough windblown debris was deposited to form the present divide between the Smoky Hill and the Arkansas, rerouting the watershed of the Smoky Hill east into the Kansas River drainage. Evidence for this shift in drainage patterns is documented in the fish fauna of both Blood and Deception creeks, the present-day remnants of that Pleistocene watershed. Fish collections in these streams revealed species known to the Smoky Hill drainage, but not the Arkansas River; other species in these creeks were found only in the Arkansas and not the Smoky Hill. The reduction in the volume of water in the ancient stream permitted the deposition of sediments, and the stream channel became filled with alluvial debris. During this time, the winds formed sand dunes on the east and southeast that enclosed the basin, fed now only by the meager flows of Blood and Deception creeks. The development of Cheyenne Bottoms had begun.

Mammals populate the Miocene savannas in the basin of Cheyenne Bottoms, herbivores like horses, peccaries, rhinoceros, and a shovel-toothed

elephant. A saber-toothed cat rests, satiated by a previous visitor to the water hole.

The record of the Bottoms begins about 100,000 years ago, near the end of the last interglacial stage. In a short time, geologically speaking, the fourth of the glaciers that characterized the Pleistocene would grind south once again but leave its terminal moraines far to the north of Cheyenne Bottoms along what is now the Missouri River in the Dakotas. During its first 30,000 years or so, the Bottoms was wet; a core of the sediments made in 1946 brought up blue gray silts, sands, and clays with mollusk fragments from this level. At the top of these deposits, however, the sediments change from blue gray to brown, indicative of drying and the development of terrestrial soil about 50,000 years ago. Another wetland period of about 30,000 years followed, but it appeared to have been intermittent, with darker zones interrupting the blue gray silts and clays. These darker layers yielded fragments of marsh plants and charcoal, the marshes periodically becoming dry enough to burn. Based on the decay rate of radioactive carbon, a date of about 30,000 years ago has been obtained from the middle of this layer in a core obtained in 1985. Fossil cattail pollen has also been recovered from this depth and recurs in subsequent periods of wetland development. Waterbirds like eared grebe, northern pintail, white pelican, hooded merganser, bufflehead, and coot are known from other Pleistocene deposits in central and western Kansas and certainly occurred in the Cheyenne Bottoms basin as well.

The end of the Wisconsin glacial stage is characterized in Kansas by the deposition of windblown loess, and a 15-foot thick layer of sediment reflecting this period rests in the basin of the Bottoms. But fossil algae in these silts indicate that a wetland environment persisted until the end of the Pleistocene, about 10,000 years ago. Fossil pollen analysis from the 1985 core indicates that the dominant vegetation around the Bottoms was a prairie of grasses,

American white pelicans

sage, ragweed, and goosefoot. Other fossil evidence from the general region reveals that mourning doves, upland sandpipers, and lark buntings would have been flushed from nest sites by humans crossing the prairie in search of game. Traces of spruce, pine, maple, alder, and birch pollen also occur in the sediments of the basin, suggesting that cooler, damper forests grew somewhere in the region. Perhaps they were as close as a few hundred miles, since cores from the Muscotah artesian bog in Atchison County in northeastern Kansas that date from approximately 15,000 years ago contain fragments of spruce needles. The wetland present in the basin at the end of the Pleistocene was followed by a distinct period of drying and terrestrial soil formation that has a radio-carbon date of about 9700 years ago. This climatic shift was confined not just to the region of Cheyenne Bottoms, but also characterized the entire continent. This period of elevated temperatures, the post-glacial hypsithermal, lasted for several thousand years and resulted in the migration of the grassland biome as far east as western Pennsylvania and the Mohawk valley of New York about 7000 years ago. Remnants of these prairies that were left behind after the grasslands retreated west across the Wabash River when temperatures again declined can still be found today. The most recent sediments at Cheyenne Bottoms reveal a continuation of intervals of aridity interlayered with periods of wetland development, a pattern that has continued into the present century.

3 Water

Water is peculiar stuff. Chemically, it is simple, yet water has miraculous properties that permit life to exist. The chemistry of life is performed in a milieu of water, and the adaptational sets of all living things are dedicated in various ways to obtaining and maintaining a water content of the correct quality and the proper concentration. Processed by plants, water becomes the source of the oxygen we breathe as the radiant energy of sunlight drives the photosynthetic reactions, splitting water molecules so that plants can capture the precious hydrogens while dumping the oxygen into the atmosphere. Water holds the heat that warms us in winter, and its evaporation keeps both plants and animals cool during summer's excessive heat. Water provides the matrix through which essential molecules are transported to the cells of all creatures. It has a tensile strength to bind itself together in long, minutely thin strands that reach from the roots to the top of the tallest, wind-rattled cottonwood, providing an avenue for the soil nutrients needed for the metabolic machinery of the leaves. It can be formed explosively, as in the sparkling catastrophe of the airship Hindenberg, and destroy life; or it can arise a molecule at a time as the end product in a series of reactions that rejoins hydrogen and oxygen atoms, providing the fire that gives life to both plants and animals. Since water is most dense when it is almost frozen, but less dense when it is frozen, lakes and rivers freeze from the surface down. This allows aquatic organisms to exist under the ice during the winter at higher latitudes.

Water can also be destructive. It can scour the surface of the earth, carrying away the soil that provides anchorage and nutrients to the plants upon which all life depends. It can saturate the soil and suffocate the roots of plants not adapted to its perpetual presence. Variation in its salinity can rupture the cells of plants and animals or, conversely, cause them to shrivel and shrink. It can fail in its recycling and leave regions of the Earth dry and barren, a desert where once a verdant valley "laughed and sang." The involvement of water in the tension between life and nonlife is a Dickensian dichotomy; the quantity and quality of water can provide the best of times or the worst of times.

The traditional ecological approach has been to consider wetlands as evanescent communities, existing briefly somewhere between the truly aquatic and the terrestrial. Through the process of ecological succession, wetland habitats change, and this change leads to the extirpation of some species and the invasion of others. Lakes become marshes; marshes fill and become dewatered to the point where shrubs, then trees invade. One community replaces another by slowly subverting the environment from within to change what was once open water to forest. It is true; I've seen it. Armed with tenth-meter squares for sampling the populations of plants and animals and diameter tapes to determine the sizes of trees, I, and many other ecology students, have retraced the stages of development which Frederick E. Clements and Victor E. Shelford demonstrated earlier in this century. We have seen the evidence now embedded among the railroad tracks and tank farms along the old postglacial beaches, arrayed like broad stair-steps climbing inland toward U.S. 30 south of Lake Michigan. What had been a shallow pond behind the foredune along the lakeshore at the end of the Pleistocene has become a complex beech/maple forest.

At least that's the way it seems to work east of the Mississippi where the basics of ecological theory developed in the universities at Chicago, Madison, Champaign-Urbana, and Durham. Although some ecologists disagree that wetland succession works that way in the East, it is clear to almost everybody that succession is different as we move west under the increasingly effective rainshadow of the Rocky Mountains. Ever since the Pliocene, the feast or famine of abundant rainfall and desiccating drought has affected the nature of wetlands on the plains. Here the tension between life and nonlife for organisms is confronted, resolved, or accepted: To survive here, organisms must evolve adaptive responses to variable amounts of water.

Periodic drought reverses the progression of marsh development about every five to twenty years. The drying up of surface waters allows annual plants—whose seeds make a rapid response to the newly exposed soil—grow, set fruit, and die. Surprisingly perhaps, most marsh emergents are not completely adapted to the aquatic environment; their seeds will not germinate in deep water. Rather, they require the conditions of temperature and oxygen that exposed mud provides. Thus the seeds of perennial marsh plants that have accumulated over the years in the bottom muck (like money in the bank waiting patiently for investment) also germinate. Then when rainfall returns and feeder streams flow again, the marsh is reflooded. The annuals are inundated and die, but the freshet born in the accession of rainfall stimulates the perennials; starting anew, the fringe of emergent vegetation that continues to encroach upon the water-filled basin until open water is almost obliterated by the thin sabers of the aggressive cattails.

Eventually the regeneration stage of the marsh is followed by a degeneration phase. The exact causation is not clear; it could be the senescence of the plants. In the case of some emergents, cattails, for example, it may be the impact of herbivores like muskrats or tiny caterpillars. It can be prolonged submersion by high water that depresses the vigor of even well-established marsh emergents. In any case, the marsh vegetation becomes sparser, and more open stretches of water develop, even approaching a lake in appearance. Then drought again intervenes, and with the drawdown, the marsh is reset to begin anew the same progression. This cycle goes on and on for a long, long time. Cheyenne Bottoms has been a wetland, off and on, for 100,000 years! The riparian woodland it ought to become, and yet still might, is no closer to fruition than it was at the end of the Pleistocene.

When ornithology was listed among the biology requirements for secondary education students at Kansas State, I frequently taught the course during the summer session. We usually spent a day at the Bottoms after it became too hot for much productive field work in the Flint Hills. But life in the Bottoms would be in full swing then, and either Ed Martinez or Marvin Schwilling would know of a Virginia rail nest in the marsh or a scrape where the least tern had its eggs. In 1967 we arrived after nocturnal thunderstorms had dropped several inches of rain in the basin, and as we waded through the marsh, the surface flow was quite noticeable and frequently carried bobbing eggs of night-herons from nests flooded by the rise in the water. The downpour of the previous night was immediately reflected in the life of the marsh as the herons filled the air, carrying sticks to start new nests so that the advent

Black-crowned night-heron

of the next generation would be assured in spite of this momentary interruption in reproduction. But that rainfall was nothing compared to the deluge during two days in August 1927 when over 14 inches of rain fell, and the basin became filled overnight to form a vast lake, lapping at the foundations of barns and houses built around its margin.

The drought of the late 1980s began with the failure of seasonal rainfall during the summer of 1988, and a dry winter was followed by an even drier spring in central Kansas. On the last day of April 1989 when I arrived with a group of students, twenty-five years after my first spring visit, the Bottoms was dry. I found out from Gene Lewis, who was leading a group from the Topeka Audubon Society, that two days previously there had been enough water to support about 50,000 shorebirds. As the water disappeared, so did the birds. It was quite fortuitous that Gonzalo Castro of Colorado State University had begun a study of fat levels in the shorebirds using the Bottoms that spring, and he was able to document the impact of this failure of habitat on the birds. His work revealed that the birds' truncated stay contributed to their leaving with lower than normal fat levels. This meant that they would be able to migrate a shorter than usual distance, perhaps only hundreds of miles instead of over a thousand, before stopping again to replenish energy stores. Thus the timing of their migratory journey could be extended, which might lead to their missing the short window of suitability of habitat on their arctic nesting grounds, preventing reproduction that year. Even if they got there on time, their lowered nutritional state might preempt any breeding activity.

The water level in Cheyenne Bottoms is clearly dependent upon rainfall, either directly or through runoff. Some of the runoff simply flows across the surface of the

Moisture from the Gulf, coalesced in the towering ferocity of a fierce prairie thunderstorm, keeps hope alive in the marsh, enthralled by the desiccating heat of summer.

ground, entering the Bottoms where it can. The other source of natural inflow is through Deception and Blood creeks, which run southeast on either side of the town of Hoisington before disappearing into the Bottoms. According to the tales told, Blood Creek received its name after a fracas that occurred around 1825 between Cheyennes and either Kiowas or Pawnees that was sufficiently gory to color the water of the creek. Normally its 61-square-mile basin provides so little water that it seldom flows at all, running only during the spring melt and after significant precipitation. Deception Creek, with a basin of only 44 square miles, has even less effect on the Bottoms. Inputs from these creeks, on average, provide less than twenty percent of the total that comes from direct precipitation.

Studies of the water balance at Cheyenne Bottoms conducted during the assessment survey substantiate what is suggested from casual observation. Precipitation is the only important source of water, and evaporation from the vegetation and the surface of the water is the major route of export. Only a small amount of water is lost through deep drainage to the water table. The evapotranspiration of water escaping from the emergent vegetation actually accounts for essentially all the precipitation, so that the evaporation from open water, which can be as much as 60 inches a year, results in an overall deficit. The volume of standing water decreases; moisture in exposed soil is sucked out. Hence, even during times of adequate rainfall, evaporation increases the salinity of the surface waters to around four times that acceptable for drinking water. During times when precipitation is so inadequate that it does not even come close to that lost by evaporation, the total dissolved solids can reach 8000 mg/liter, about one-fourth the salinity of the ocean. In most years as the summer progresses, almost all the water is eventually lost, and expansive areas of the marsh are dry. Even though the great rain of 1927 was followed by another year of above-average rainfall, the basin was dry by 1931. The water deficit, driven by the thirsty winds of summer, takes its toll in time. In drought years like 1989, the Bottoms is dry even before summer begins. And even though in May and June of that year rains partially refilled the basin, birds were noticeably sparce. Most birds had left earlier in response to the unsuitability of the habitat, or if they tarried, they did not breed.

Given that the water loss in the basin of Cheyenne Bottoms usually exceeds gain, it is surprising that the level of the water table under the Bottoms has not fallen below that measured forty years ago. Apparently the subsurface structure of the basin isolates this pocket of ground water from the declining levels of regional water tables. On the eastern side of the basin, which is overlain by dune sand, the infiltration of precipitation is quick and ground water movement is rapid. Over much of the Bottoms, however, the transport of water down to the water table is slow and passes through layers of saline sediments left from times past when the wetland completely evaporated. As the water seeps through this historical cross-section of successive droughts, it becomes very salty, reaching a concentration of total dissolved solids equal to about one-third the salt concentration of the ocean.

The obligatory thirst of life for water and the reality of the summer droughts, as well as the periodic failure of seasonal rainfall, affect the configuration of a wetland, generating its cyclicity. Man's intervention to maintain some particular stage in this cycle that he deems desirable or to extrinsically impose another cycle on the wetland requires circumvention of drought by water storage, supplementation, and subsequent drainage. This is the management strategy at Cheyenne Bottoms. The water income is augmented by the transfer of water from the Arkansas River and Walnut Creek through a 23-mile series of diversion dams and ditches that enter the Bottoms from the west, south of Blood Creek, feeding into a cluster of diked pools that have replaced the natural water-filled basin. At least that was the plan in 1957 when this system was completed, following the securing of surface rights for an annual total of 50,000 acre-feet from both the Arkansas River and Walnut Creek, an amount equivalent to over 1,500 tons of water.

But water is no longer readily available for diversion, especially in the summer when it is most needed to counteract evaporation. In contrast to the 1960s when from 20,000 to 70,000 acre-feet were transferred each year from the Arkansas River to the inlet canal at the Dundee diversion dam, by the early 1980s the volume had dropped to an annual average of around 4,000 acre-feet; by 1985 only 493 acre-feet were removed. Flow in Walnut Creek increases the amount that actually is directed towards the Bottoms, but this addition is still insufficient to provide enough water for any planned marsh management. Since 1980, the flow from both sources has been less than 10 percent of the legally protected amounts. Even when water is available to be diverted, considerable water is lost during the day-and-a-half travel time in the inlet canal. Frequently, as much as 80 percent of that taken from the Arkansas River never gets to the Bottoms! Some is lost through evaporation; much more is lost by seepage from the unprotected channel of the inlet canal. Nor can runoff water be stored in times of plenty. Pools within the management area are too shallow to accommodate sufficient volume, and allowing water levels to rise leads to infringement on bordering private lands and litigation. So water is released through the outlet canal and flows down Little Cheyenne Creek to Cow Creek to the Arkansas to the Mississippi to the Gulf of Mexico, far from where it is needed. Today the water balance equation for Cheyenne Bottoms lacks a significant term for supplementation.

The Bottoms is once again largely dependent on the precipitation within its basin and the watersheds of its two feeder streams, just as in the days before humankind attempted to intervene. These days are worse, however, because in earlier times when the Bottoms went dry, the Arkansas River still flowed with the snow melt from the mountains, forming braided patterns of shallow channels in the sand and silt which offered ample foraging space for hungry migrating shorebirds, probably even in late

Looking toward the Bottoms in March: damp patches in the channel of Deception Creek, remembrances of surface flows.

Black-bellied plovers

summer. Although Lieutenant Pike was not impressed with the flow in October 1806, the river was alive. Other wetlands serviced by watersheds larger than Cheyenne Bottoms and thus more resilient to drought provided additional alternate stopover habitats throughout the sand prairies in the Arkansas lowlands. But the Arkansas has had much of its surface flow rerouted through the millions of spigots in the burgeoning megalopolis at the foot of the Front Range and has been attacked from below as the water table is pulled out from under through center pivot irrigation systems. The Arkansas River no longer flows continuously. It is dead.

The same fate has befallen other watersheds, leaving no alternate habitats to supplement what the Bottoms cannot provide in times of drought, a unique event in the evolutionary history of the species. Innate memories, those traces encoded into the chemical bonds of the genetic material, have led these species unerringly during their seasonal passages through the sustenance provided by the wetlands of the Great Plains. Migratory stopover sites are essential to their existence. Indeed, the timing of their migratory journeys has evolved to allow them to take advantage of the transient suitability of these rest stops along the intercontinental highways that connect breeding grounds with contranuptial havens. What happens now? One principle of biology is that life continues in the face of secular environmental change because of the intrinsic variability built into the mechanisms of inheritance. Differences among the individuals of a species are biologically good. If environmental change is too rapid, however, outrunning the range of variation in a species' set of adaptations so that even the most eccentric individuals find life unbearable, extinction occurs. We hope that we can moderate the forces assaulting Cheyenne Bottoms in order to maintain the habitat within the range of variation of suitability for the myriad species dependent on this critically important oasis.

4 The Marsh

Dr. Frederick A. Wislizenus was not a birdwatcher. Such people did not exist in 1839 when he became lost in the fog on October 28 with his riding horse, his pack horse, and his dog and stumbled into "a great swamp" that was Cheyenne Bottoms, an incident that seems more appropriate on the road to Casterbridge than on the Kansas prairie. But it was the birds that he wrote about: "Never have I seen together such quantities of swans, cranes, pelicans, geese and ducks, as were here." A century and a half ago the birds were notable, and still today Cheyenne Bottoms would be much less impressive without them. This wetland would be nothing but a soggy patch of ground, a morass, if it were not for its attraction as an oasis in a parched and wind-seared landscape, beckoning the greatest travelers on the globe. Marco Polo seeking refuge at Turfan after circumnavigating the Takla Makan Depression pales to the insignificant compared to these migrants for whom a trip between the tip of South America to some tiny speck in the arctic archipelago is a twice-annual event. And they come to the Bottoms by the thousands.

On my first visit to the Bottoms in 1955, however, I did not see any birds. In fact, the visit was illegal. My instructor pilot's current girl friend lived in Great Bend. On the return leg to Enid, Oklahoma, from a cross-country flight to Denver we "buzzed" her house and then continued northeast out of town, low across the marsh so that "no one would get our number." Ours was probably not the first military aircraft to make a low pass across the Bottoms; the area had been used as a bombing and gunnery range a decade earlier. I did not see the Bottoms again until the spring of 1964, my first year on the faculty at Kansas State University. I was surprised. I had birded many wetlands, but I had never experienced one where the birds were so highly concentrated and so accessible. Thousands of dowitchers were arrayed across the mudflats, their probing bills like sewing machine needles busily knitting up the bottom of the marsh as if to prevent any further loss of water. The turnstones and knots of Delaware Bay and the semipalmated sandpipers in the Bay of Fundy also offer comparable panoramas of abundance, but few other sites east of the Rocky Mountains are as spectacular as these. At Cheyenne Bottoms tens of thousands of Baird's sandpipers and other "peeps" compete for space among the dowitchers. And when the migration of Baird's sandpipers subsides, they are replaced in the following weeks with even larger numbers of white-rumped sandpipers. Scores of avocets scythe the shallows, hundreds of phalaropes spin up whirlpools from the bottom, and white pelicans paddle in tightening crescents, communally fishing for young carp.

The images of Cheyenne Bottoms change as the march of the seasons parades diverse species through the marsh. As soon as the first warmth of February begins to divest the pools of ice, the geese drop through the furrows in the banks of stratocumulus to offer variety to the hoards of blackbirds roosting in the cattails during the cold of winter. Speckle-bellied white fronts and Canadas in three sizes are joined by fast flying phalanxes of pintails and tight bunches of green-winged teal. In mid-March, an

Long-billed dowitchers avidly restore fat spent in last night's flight from the Texas coast at the expense of bloodworms hiding in the muck.

hour before daybreak, hundreds of sandhill cranes are clustered just offshore in the central pool. In the gray, colorless dimness of predawn, they rise in groups, bugling in guttural trills, as they depart for the great staging grounds on the Platte. Even then the vanguard of the sandpipers appears, soon followed in April by tens of thousands of their kin arriving in thick-packed skeins, rushing across the marsh on the strong southerly wind like wisps of low scud, exposing their white bellies in unison as they hook around to approach upwind and settle at last among the feeding flocks.

Summer is heron time; even the reclusive least bittern announces its abundance by frequent trips across the clattering cattails carrying food to its young. Late summer is dying time; the stench of decaying fish permeates the air,

During March and October sandhill cranes find a roosting haven in the marsh between daytime visits to upland pastures and cropland.

but the reduced pools concentrate the first shorebirds fleeing aborted nesting attempts on the arctic tundra. As long as the moisture holds, the waterbirds come. Western sandpipers looping south through the Great Plains are now abundant enough that comparisons of their plumage variations can be made with the equally varied semipalmated sandpipers. Now is a time for the unusual: red knots and small flocks of red-necked phalaropes, the lone Sabine's gull. One day a family of whooping cranes stops on its way to the marshes on Aransas Bay.

If the water is still in the Bottoms in fall and winter, the ducks and geese congregate on the refuge pools. Some sacrifice their lives to repay the debt to the hunters who purchased this stopping place with excise taxes on guns and ammunition. Bald eagles concentrate, roosting in nearby windbreaks, while a few ferruginous hawks arrive to await mid-winter excursions by prairie dogs from their burrows. Most of the waterfowl pass on as winter begins to solidify its hold, but a few geese linger. Northern harriers transect the marsh in search of rodents who are now scampering exposed, hurrying to gather forage before the time of cold and deprivation. Then the kaleidoscope of the turning seasons rests again in the depth of winter when superabundant red-wings, their scarlet epaulets subdued by the postnuptial molt, hunch down as wind-driven snow sifts through the cattails and keep warm through the metabolism of cattle food purloined from local feedlots.

A CORNERSTONE FOR THE ECOSYSTEM

It is not just water that attracts; the birds are there because food is there. Cheyenne Bottoms, like all marshes, is a system that lives on decay. Life arises from the muck of the marsh and to the muck it does return. A marsh, perhaps more obviously than any other ecological community, of-

With a sharp eye, the northern harrier scans the edge of the marsh for the telltale scurrying of potential prey through the stems of saltgrass.

fers a continuing liturgy whose rubrics direct the flow of energy and the cycling of matter through death and resurrection. The cornerstone species in this construct of relationships are the insignificant chironomids (midges), whose swarms in summer infest the heads of heedless intruders and whose larvae, the bloodworms, live in the detritus on the bottom of the marsh. They are blood red because of the high concentration of hemoglobin in their bodies, which allows them to scavenge the limited oxygen in this soup of sludge where they live and have their being. They convert death into life. They burrow in the sediment or build tubes of mud, casting nets or strings of sticky saliva from their mouths to sweep the interface between water and bottom, gathering bacteria-infested organic debris and its encrustations of microscopic, one-celled diatoms.

This stuff is the remnant of complex structures that once blew into the prairie wind from the flowering heads of cattails, or pulled the rack and pinion of contractile proteins to shorten the muscles that propelled carp through murky channels, or was imported to the Bottoms from northern bogs within the keratinaceous fabric of yellow-legs' wings. Multitudes of creatures, some as large as muskrats but most much smaller, burrow, scrape, crunch, shred, and munch, converting these structures into bits and pieces, which in turn are attacked by the fungi and bacteria. The midge larvae take these remnants and restructure that matter into bloodworm protoplasm. And it's bloodworm protoplasm for which the sandpipers have come after trekking north from beyond the Tropic of Capricorn and upon which they feed and grow fat before again stretching their long, pointed wings for one last, nonstop, two-thousand-mile journey toward the Arctic Circle. What these bloodworms do not use is egested; this excrement, in turn, can be absorbed directly by the roots

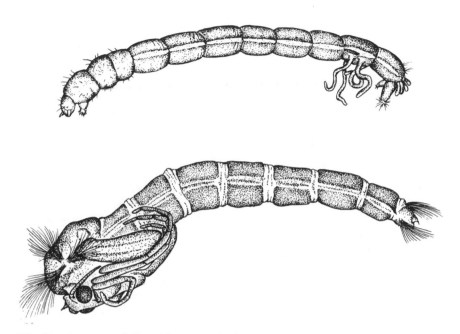

The bloodworm and the midge pupa fuel intercontinental journeys.

of plants or undergo further microbial degradation into compounds that can then be taken up by plants, entering again into the food web.

Midges are everywhere in Cheyenne Bottoms. Some species even get a leg up on the competition through a little insider trading by burrowing into the stems and leaves of cattails. But most rely on a trickle-down economy, waiting in the water or, far more frequently, on the bottom for the fragments from the sun-drenched world of production above. Through all seasons of the year, the highest densities of midge larvae are found in the submerged mud flats, those stretches of muck covered by a shallow veneer of water. In June there can be as many as 65,082 bloodworms per square meter; that's about 50 larvae per square inch. Wayne Hoffman calculated the total

45

area of the various aquatic habitats at Cheyenne Bottoms; having computed the density of bloodworm larvae in each habitat and the mass of the average larva's protoplasm (some are over an inch long), he determined the total mass of bloodworm protoplasm available as bird food. From March through November the submerged mud flat habitat shelters an average mass (dry weight) of 55,045 kilograms per month. That's 61 tons of food available every month from early spring to late fall and represents over three-fourths of the total mass of bloodworms available at the Bottoms.

Not surprisingly, most of the shorebirds and many of the waterfowl that pass through prefer this habitat or mudflats recently exposed. In the early spring, the larger dabbling ducks feed on the pupae and the newly emerged adults that survived the winter as larvae. Later migrants, like shovelers, paddle along over the submerged flats, their heads under water, sifting the bottom sludge with their spatula-shaped bills to extract the bloodworms. They are usually accompanied by blue-winged teal, which supplement a diet of seeds with the abundant midge larvae. The green-winged teal feed here as well, but prefer to gather food on newly exposed mud, searching for prey visually. The plovers, both the smaller-bodied snowy, piping, and semipalmated as well as the larger black-bellied and golden, also feed on the exposed mud. Here they stand and watch, and then chase after the prey in a rapid run to catch a squirming morsel in their short, stout bills. Most of the small sandpipers, however, are more probabilistic in their search for food, probing the mud with a thin bill, trying by chance to find a bloodworm by means of the touch receptors packed into the sensitive tip. With a density of 50 worms per square inch, the birds don't miss too often. But the bloodworm-eaters don't get it all. The populations of shorebirds in April and May, when their impact on the bloodworms is maximal, still represent an estimated biomass that is only 7 to 11 percent of the biomass of their chironomid prey. Such a ratio reflects sustainability in the exploitation of this resource; many bloodworms survive, ensuring that a subsequent generation will follow.

Midge larvae can also withstand the climatic rigors of Cheyenne Bottoms. Larvae of some species still remained alive after being stored in dry soil for as long as four years in the laboratory, and many species in nature regularly withstand the seasonal dry periods that eliminate the ponds and pools in which they hatched. Midges have a life cycle similar to that of the butterfly. The bloodworm is the "caterpillar," and like the caterpillar, it enters into a stage in which it does not feed but metamorphoses into the adult insect. For the midge, this pupal stage lasts just a short time, a week in the cool of spring, only a day in summer. Then shortly before sunset, the pupa leaves the bottom of the marsh and swims to the surface. The adult midge emerges from a slit along the back of its pupal case in less than a minute, rests momentarily on the surface tension, and then flies away. Adults do not feed; they live but a few days.

If the midge is a male, at dawn, at dusk, and sometimes during mid-day, he will join with other males in large, single-sex swarms sometimes containing as many as 20,000 to 40,000 individuals. These swarms are oriented over contrastingly colored objects on the ground—a galvanized stock tank in a pasture, a pale rock pile in a green field, quite frequently along the light-colored roadways on the dikes that border the marsh at Cheyenne Bottoms. All the males face the same way, darting into the wind, drifting back, then flying into the wind again, holding their positions in the swarm even at wind velocities up to 20 miles per hour.

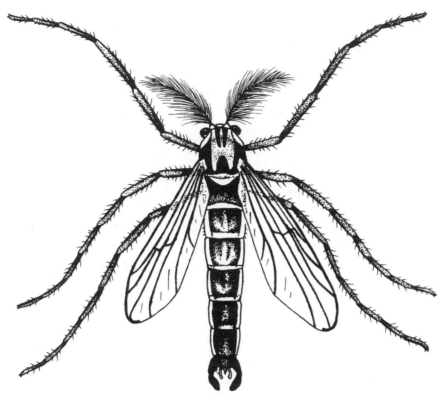

Adult midge

When the female is ready to mate, she enters the swarm in the early morning and is seized around the thorax by one of the males. They drop down, typically concluding copulation even before they reach the ground. There they may remain attached end to end, but soon they separate; the male reenters the swarm, and the female flies away to remain quiescent for about a day and a half. Then an inner urge arises in the small cluster of nerve cells embracing her esophagus that functions as a brain, causing her to make one last flight over the water. The fertilized eggs are extruded from her abdomen in a gelatinous mass containing from one thousand to two thousand embryos.

She dips down to the surface of the water and releases the egg mass. She flies on a little farther, settles onto the water's surface herself, and dies. Her egg mass absorbs water, swells in size, and sinks to the protection of the bottom, ensuring that midges will swarm again, perhaps in just several weeks, or if it is autumn, the next year. Depending on the temperature, the eggs soon hatch into larvae which eat the gelatinous matrix in which they developed. Then they are dispersed by water currents throughout the marsh, where they settle down to the business of eating from the banquet of death and decay that drizzles down in their midst.

AN EDDY CURRENT IN THE SOLAR TORRENT

Death and decay follow life, and life at Cheyenne Bottoms, like life everywhere on this planet, is ultimately dependent on that thermonuclear furnace lying 93 million miles "above" the Earth that converts 600 million tons of hydrogen into helium every second. The resulting radiation crosses the abyss of space, raining the full spectrum of its energy toward the planet, but only about half the radiation actually reaches the surface of the Earth. Even then, some of this energy is too intense for capture into the chemical bonds that hold the atoms of biologically important compounds together (in fact, it will destroy these bonds), and some of the energy is too weak. Only the red and blue wavelengths of the visible spectrum can be used by plants, so that just a quarter of the ground-level radiation energy has the potential for incorporation into living protoplasm. Maximum production by the best domestic crops converts only 3 to 14 percent of the total radiation incident upon their leaves into calories of plant tissue. Transduction of the light energy of sunlight into the chemical energy within most plant bodies is generally much lower than this. Yet this minuscule input of energy floods the biosphere with sufficient power to drive life and provide for the natural recycling of matter. Life dips into the stream of solar energy intercepted by the planet rotating along its revolutionary path and creates order from disorder, seeming to postpone for a while the inevitability of the Second Law of Thermodynamics on this one small mote within the system of the sun and producing a spectacular diversity of creatures and intricacies of relationships that are fitting reflections of the supernal.

Wetlands like the Bottoms are but a minute facet of the biosphere encrusting the surface of the planet, yet they scintillate with an energetic intensity out of proportion to their spatial contribution to the blue jewel in the cosmos called Earth. In his study of the Cheyenne Bottoms' ecosystem, Wayne Hoffman determined that cattails growing in flooded pools produce about 9.75 kilograms of matter on every square meter of surface during the growing season, while those growing on drained soils produce just 30 percent of that, or 2.9 kilograms per square meter. During the wetter year of the two-year assessment study, 79 percent of the cattails were flooded, while in the drier year, only 34 percent of the cattails were growing in standing water. Thus, in wet years, on average across the marsh, every square meter of cattails produces about 8.3 kilograms of matter, while during dry years this value is 5.2 kilograms. These numbers are from two to three times greater than the maximum for narrow-leaved cattail measured in other mid-latitude freshwater marshes, and two to almost four times greater than the production of *Spartina* grass in salt marshes.

Similar values for the average crop production in the central United States, on the other hand, are about one and one-half times greater than that of the cattails during dry years but equal to cattail production in wet years.

Even if the values for cattail production at Cheyenne Bottoms represent only two years' data and perhaps were subject to sampling errors in their measurement, the magnitude implied is still impressive. The level of production by the cattails denotes a conversion efficiency of incoming solar radiation of 1.2 percent in dry years and 1.9 in wet years. Salt marshes do only about half as well at 0.8 percent, but tallgrass prairie shows a dismal 0.1 percent. In fact, the cattails at Cheyenne Bottoms compare favorably to the efficiency of corn, which usually converts 1 percent of the incoming solar radiation into the energy contained within corn protoplasm and seldom exceeds 2 percent. Considering that corn has been artificially selected by man since before the beginning of our written history and recognizing the years and years of well-funded technological efforts to improve productivity, it is amazing that cattails have attained a comparable level of efficiency simply through natural selection and the fortunate luxury of living in a habitat in which the necessities of life are usually superabundant.

Perhaps this high-energy efficiency is the basis for narrow-leaved cattail being the dominant plant at Cheyenne Bottoms today. This was not always so. When the first vegetative survey was conducted in June 1929 by F. W. Uhler and F. A. Warren, no species of cattails were mentioned, even though *Typha* pollen is present in cores of Pleistocene bottom sediments. Their work was done after the great rain of 1927 had refilled a dry basin, starting anew the characteristic cyclic pattern of drought-impacted prairie wetlands. Thus the ecological community sampled by Uhler and Warren was a "young" community, composed of scattered stands of bulrush with spikesedge bordering almost the entire edge of the main pool of open water. Additional wetland species like dock, barnyard grass, smartweeds, and arrowhead occurred. The studies by two graduate students from Fort Hays State University, D. Sonnenberg in 1961 and D. W. Hastings in 1970, described a floristic composition that reflected further successional development and the initial appearance of both narrow-leaved and broad-leaved cattail, but neither of these species was important in the community. The recent invasion of the narrow-leaved cattail is not unique to Cheyenne Bottoms. Prior to 1950 the species was rare in Kansas, but by 1977 its presence had been documented in every county. This explosive spread has covered a broad geographic area and established this native of the northeastern corner of the North American continent throughout the Great Plains.

The increase in cattail has been at the expense of bulrushes, which are now confined to small stands at the periphery of the cattail belt or to small patches in open water. These plants, spikesedge (which now occurs in shallow depressions beyond the cattails), and other wetland species contribute their share to the capture of solar energy. Unlike other wetlands, however, the submerged vegetation here is sparse and contributes little to the marsh ecosystem because the shallowness of the pools combined with the almost constant wind that pushes and roils the water disturbs the rooting of submerged plants and keeps the water constantly turbid, preventing sufficient penetration by light. Uhler and Warren commented on the relationship of wave action to the scarcity of submerged vegetation, and this physical characteristic of the Cheyenne Bottoms environment continues to have a significant effect. For this same reason, energy capture by algae and photosynthetic bacteria is limited, and thus these organisms are not an important component of the flora.

Other groups of plants that contribute to the photosynthetic productivity of Cheyenne Bottoms are those that take advantage of the extensive barren flats that become exposed through the evaporative drawdown of the pools first formed in the spring. By mid-summer, kochia, aster, snow-on-the-mountain, pigweed, goosefoot, barnyard grass, smartweeds, and other annuals have germinated and covered the exposed soil with a rank growth.

UP THE CONSUMER PATHWAY

The energy, carbon dioxide, and various mineral nutrients that are fixed in the structures of the organic compounds synthesized by the green plants, the primary producers, have just two fates. Either they are eaten by animals or, after the death of the plants, they enter the detritivore-decomposer pathway, a system of organisms ranging in complexity from carp and crayfish down to bacteria and fungi. In freshwater marshes, 90 percent of the total production of green plants moves down this latter route, through the organisms that convert dead plant matter into fragments and eventually into simpler inorganic nutrients. Only a tenth of the flow of energy and matter takes the former route, moving up against this cascade to fuel the lives of the herbivores that feed upon the plants and the carnivores that in turn feed upon them. Although this initial bifurcation in the energy-matter pathways is simple enough, subsequent patterns reveal a network of routes that interconnect the herbivore-carnivore pathway with that of the detritivores and decomposers, forming what can be described best as a food web.

Cattails are the dominant primary producers, and only two organisms have a major role in moving matter and energy up this down staircase by feeding on cattails. One is a small, white moth (*Simyra henrici*), related to the corn borer. The caterpillar feeds on the shoots and can convert the green blanket of cattails into a yellow pall over hundreds of acres of marsh. Although no quantitative values

As marsh engineer, the muskrat is a keystone species in the functioning of the community.

have been obtained at Cheyenne Bottoms, an ecologically similar moth that infested an average of 10 percent of the stems of the cattails in a Minnesota marsh caused a 45 percent decrease in productivity of the affected shoots.

The other cattail feeder is the muskrat, which not only devours the rootstocks, but uses the stems to construct its lodge in deeper parts of the marsh. Indeed, shallow water limits the presence of muskrats, since the water must be deep enough to permit the movement of the animals into and out of their lodges when the surface is covered by ice. At Cheyenne Bottoms water of sufficient depth occurs only along the barrows bordering the dikes, and in drier years these are often too shallow. Not only do lowered water levels limit muskrats, but in the absence of large predators like wolves and cougars, disease also exerts biological control on the population. In May 1986 during the assessment study, muskrats became scarce, and rotted carcasses were found in the marsh. This decrease was coincident with a decrease in the striped skunk population and, given the abnormal behavior noted for the skunks, suggests that a contagious disease depressed both populations. The reduction in muskrat populations is unfortunate since it has been shown for marshes formed in the deep glacial lakes of Iowa that a sufficiently large population of muskrats keeps the marsh from becoming clogged with cattails. A coverage of about one-half cattail and one-half open water results in maximum diversity and abundance of invertebrates and appears to be the configuration most preferred by waterfowl. Although some muskrats construct their lodges as burrows in the dikes that confine the pools at Cheyenne Bottoms, those that do build lodges of vegetation within the interior of the marsh provide loitering sites and nest platforms for geese and many duck species. Wayne Hoffman identified the muskrat as one of the critical populations of Cheyenne Bottoms, a keystone species whose presence is manifest through a wide range of ecological relationships.

Annual plants transfer much of their photosynthetic production into the seeds, which guarantee their continued existence in future generations long after their leaves and stems have withered away. Since these seeds are a concentrated food source for animals, far better than the low energy, low digestibility offered by leaves, a wide range of animals have evolved specializations for seed eating—beetles like weevils, rodents like kangaroo rats, harvest mice, voles, and a whole guild of sparrows and buntings. The annuals that invade exposed flats during the summer drawdown at Cheyenne Bottoms become a valuable food source for waterfowl when these areas are reflooded, either by human manipulation of water levels or from the onset of fall rains. The seeds of plants like kochia, dock, barnyard grass, and smartweed are important for a number of herbivorous waterbirds like white-fronted geese, northern pintails, blue-winged teal, coots, sora rails, and sandhill cranes. Other waterfowl like Canada geese, gadwall, and American wigeon graze directly on the leaves of annual plants but feed on domestic winter wheat when available rather than on natural vegetation.

As matter and the chemical energy it contains move up from producer to herbivore to carnivore, the total quantity available at each level decreases. This pattern is often described as being pyramidal, a broad base of energy made available by the producers, a narrower level representing the energy in the herbivores, and a pinnacle depicting the energy in the carnivores. Most of the energy ingested by herbivores, for example, is used for their own maintenance. Life does not negate the Second Law of Thermodynamics. The synthesis of an enzyme that allows the muskrat to digest cattail tissue, the secretion of a hormone that mobilizes stored fats in times of stress, the contraction of a muscle, the replication of a gene, indeed every reaction that occurs within the body of a muskrat produces heat along with work. That heat is lost to the muskrat and to the ecosystem, eventually being radiated to the blackness of deep space. Energy and matter cannot be created or destroyed but can be converted into other forms. One form of energy is unusable, because animals cannot eat heat. Matter is lost too; food parts not eaten and the organic wastes of both digestion and metabolism pass to the detritivores and decomposers. The textbook rule of thumb suggests that only about 10 percent of the energy in the plants is available to the herbivores, which in turn provide only 10 percent of the energy in their biomass for the carnivores.

There are few carnivores because the resources to support them are limited by the losses at each level of the energy pyramid. This scarcity is especially true in marsh

Elegant mink, rapacious carnivore

ecosystems where a very large share of the primary production moves down through the detrivores and decomposers. Of course, that pathway has its own carnivores; in
fact, because of the quantity of input, that system has
more steps with carnivores in turn eating carnivores. Yet
their numbers are reduced the farther along they operate
in the food web. At Cheyenne Bottoms the upward path
is short; the mink stands almost alone as carnivore, feeding primarily on herbivorous small mammals and muskrats. Omnivorous raccoons also share the feast, frequently
plundering nests of birds, and snapping turtles capture
both adult and especially young waterbirds as they swim
through the marsh. Small mammals are taken during the
day by northern harriers and at night by great horned
owls; the opportunistic massasauga rattler adds small
mammals to its diet whenever it can. All of these predators seek alternate prey in the detritivore food web, a

choice the mink often disdains, except for an occasional crayfish or small carp.

Close encounters with predators are rare because of their low numbers, but perhaps because of our fascination with the violence of their lifestyle, or perhaps because of the perceived majesty of their demeanor, such encounters are memorable. For a couple of years I was doing a survey of rails in eastern Kansas. This is most effectively done by playing tape recordings of their calls and noting the responding calls of the birds, since rails are more easily heard than seen. In April and May the rails were quite vociferous, but by June I could no longer get a response. To determine whether the birds had migrated farther north or whether they had just become more taciturn with the beginning of the breeding season, I went to Cheyenne Bottoms where I knew rails nested to play my tapes. At the west end of the central pool there is a peninsular dike that juts out into the marsh like a finger, surrounded on both sides by good stands of cattail. Getting rails to respond is best done in the hour before dawn, so I arrived early on a rare, cool, windless morning, playing the call of a Virginia rail and having birds "grunting" back to me from the cattails. It is not unusual for the rails to move out of the cattails and come almost to your feet as they investigate the source of the newcomer they now hear in their midst, and out of the corner of my eye something low and dark emerged into the open. But it was quite unraillike as it slunk toward me along the water's edge. It was followed by another, and then others, until four young mink, trailed by what I assumed to be the female, came closer and closer by successive leaps. Although within 10 feet, they acted oblivious to my presence. They most assuredly smelled me at that close range, but with regal self-assurance, they unhurriedly crossed over the dike to the other side and disappeared into the cattails. Perhaps they occasionally pounce on calling rails and were disappointed in what they found.

ASHES TO ASHES, MUCK TO MUCK

There's a stink about a marsh. It's a musky smell, a seductive smell, a smell of organic richness. Sewers and rotten eggs alone do not smell good; but a marsh smells good. I sometimes wonder if the appeal of the odor of the marsh is not some sort of atavistic recall in the biochemical essence of our being, since marshes smell like the whole world must have smelled during the first billion or so years after life began. On the early Earth, photosynthetic organisms had not yet evolved and hence there was no free oxygen in the atmosphere. Similarly, there is scant free oxygen in the sodden soil that supports life in the marsh. The environment is reductive, that is, hydrogen, not oxygen, is the element that combines with other elements. Anaerobic organisms in this deep, dark muck produce methane (sewer gas) instead of carbon dioxide, hydrogen sulfide (rotten eggs) instead of sulfates, ammonia (dirty diapers) instead of nitrates. These gases bubble up in the marsh, reeking of life different from the eolian world of human existence. From Macbeth's encounter with the three hags who "hover through the fog and filthy air" to the late show featuring the monster from the black lagoon, marshy lands engender visions of the underworld and the occult.

In reality, marshes not only smell good, they are good. They are sponges that retain water, allowing it to seep down to replenish the ground water rather than hurtling seaward in a mad rush across the landscape in channels often made straight by misguided technocrats. Marshes are filters, not only permitting soil particles to settle out, but also actively trapping products of our technological society. Heavy metals from industrial and agricultural sources form insoluble combinations with the organic molecules that dominate the sludge; nitrates and phosphates that enter waters from both agricultural and domestic activities are similarly transformed into less available compounds or are transferred through biological uptake into the vegetation growing in the marsh. Marshes are natural recycling systems that cleanse the water and make essential materials integral to life available again. This comes to pass through the many and varied activities of the organisms that constitute the detritivore-decomposer pathway.

The senescence of cattails begins in the early fall. Over two-thirds of the nitrogen, phosphorous, and potassium is translocated from the leaves to the underground stems (rhizomes) before the first frost kills the parts above ground. Although some of these elements are retained for growth in the following spring, a substantial portion is lost from the rootstock by leaching into the water-saturated soil. The standing dead stalks of cattails, the remnants remaining after infestation by cattail moths, and other dying perennial emergents and annual plants continue to lose remaining nutrients as bacteria proliferate in their lifeless structures, secreting enzymes that digest their tissues. Fall and winter rains trickle down the vulnerable shoots, carrying away soluble organic compounds to the water below. Eventually the dead stalks of vegetation fall into the water under continued attack from the physical effects of wind, rain, snow, and ice as well as from the biotic environment.

The degradation of plant structure does not end once the plant is entombed in the water, for now it is accessible to the two major plant scavengers, crayfish and turtles, especially the abundant painted turtles, which convert

Basking in the morning sun, a painted turtle gains heat before returning to the cold waters of the April marsh.

this material into even smaller bits and pieces as they claw, tear, and chew, ingesting what they need for food. Furthermore, throughout the entire growing season, substantial additions to the plant scavengers' larder come from the fragments of cattails harvested but not eaten by muskrats. All the while, the billions of plant cells disrupted by all this munching and crunching ooze organic compounds into the sludge at the bottom of the marsh. Everywhere, on still recognizable plant parts as well as on degraded debris, the ubiquitous and superabundant bacteria continue to feast on this wealth of detritus. The bacteria, in turn, provide a food source for a whole assemblage of animals known as roundworms (nematodes) of which we know almost nothing. Yet they must play essential roles as bacteria-feeders in the detritivore pathway since at their population peak in April they make up

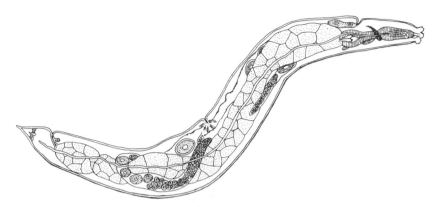

Free-living nematodes feed on the abundant bacteria that infest the marsh. Enlarged 75 times.

around 25 percent of the total invertebrate fauna found in the submerged mud at Cheyenne Bottoms, exceeding the number of bloodworms by a factor of two.

As pools evaporate during the heat of summer, raccoons provide an important step in the detritivore-decomposer pathway as they scavenge the carcasses of carp, competing with fly maggots for the compounds essential to life. Other carnivores, like coyotes, move into the marsh to take advantage of easily obtainable, though putrid, flesh. In winter bald eagles come south, concentrating around the Bottoms to feast on carrion, both fish and fowl, although they do take live fish as long as the water stays open. Death under the water provides sustenance for the most abundant snake at Cheyenne Bottoms, the diamond-backed water snake, an important scavenger of dead fish and frogs. Painted turtles, the second most abundant reptile at the Bottoms, also partition their diet about fifty-fifty between plant remains and carrion. All the animals of the marsh, no matter what their position in the food web, contribute to the nutrient pool through the defecation of undigested food, the excretion of the waste products of their internal metabolism, and ultimately their own death.

Through death, decay, and the activities of scavengers, a rich stew of plant and animal detritus, particulate organic matter, soluble compounds, and dissolved nutrients forms on the bottom of the marsh. Into this flocculate of sludge the carp comes. It is well adapted to this habitat since it has a low metabolic rate and thus is tolerant of the low oxygen levels that occur there. It also depends on smell and taste rather than on sight to find its food in this murky environment. Many fishes use swim bladders to adjust their buoyancy, but the carp's swim bladder is used as a sensitive sound receptor, sending vibrations through a series of small bones to its inner ear for transmission to hearing centers in its brain. Like other vertebrates living in turbid aquatic habitats, hearing becomes more important than sight in getting about and avoiding predators. Rooting around on the bottom like an aquatic pig, the carp sucks up the silty sludge by the mouthful, then spits it out and selects bloodworms and other insect larvae, small crustaceans, and snails, but a great deal of plant material and unrecognizable detritus gets into its gut as well. On this diet, the carp grow large, large enough and abundant enough to attract anglers and provide the only significant fisheries at the Bottoms.

The carp is native to Asia, where it has been cultivated for centuries as a food fish. This fish-farming technology had been transferred to Europe, and carp were well known to European immigrants coming to North America, especially to the Great Plains, in the late nineteenth century. Concerned about the declining stocks of native river and lake fishes resulting from intense commercial exploitation and increasing urbanization and industrialization, President Ulysses S. Grant appointed a commission

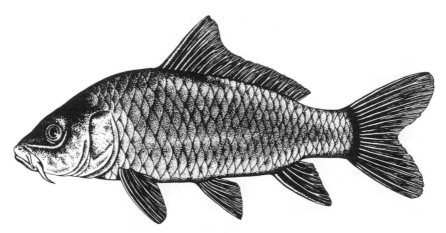

The carp, plodding plowman of the bottom muck

in 1871 to oversee the nation's fisheries and to consider possible introduction of exotic fishes to augment the supply of food fishes. Spencer Fullerton Baird, a member of this commission, championed the carp because of its hardiness and adaptability to a wide range of water conditions, its fecundity, its harmlessness to other fish species, and its good table qualities.

Time would only tell whether these arguments were valid, but by 1877 Baird had convinced the commission of the carp's admirable attributes, and a program of introduction was begun. The first carp were released in Kansas in 1880. Elliot Coues, the narrator of Pike's journey who associated the explorer with Cheyenne Bottoms, named the Baird's sandpiper after Spencer Fullerton Baird in 1861. The Baird's sandpiper is one of the species whose hemispheric population is closely allied to the continuance of Cheyenne Bottoms. The well being of many other species at the Bottoms, in turn, is closely allied to the carp, especially young carp, since they are an important food for carnivorous fishes like the green sunfish, for the diamond-backed water snake and the northern water snake, the double-crested cormorant, and for osprey, raccoon, and mink. The presence of large numbers of American white pelicans, obvious to even the most casual visitor to Cheyenne Bottoms, appears to be especially dependent on the abundance of juvenile carp.

The carp could move into environments like Cheyenne Bottoms and carve out a way of life for itself, but native fishes are similarly adapted to the high turbidity, low oxygen concentration, and silty substrate offered by the Bottoms. The most abundant fish in the waters of Cheyenne Bottoms is the fathead minnow, which feeds on a variety of plant and animal matter, algae, and organic detritus. The fathead is a pioneer species, the first to invade intermittent creeks after rains have produced flow, and the last to disappear as pools dry up under the drought of summer. Thus the stringent conditions of the Bottoms suit it quite well. If water remains, the minnows live for about three years. A female may spawn more than twelve times in a single summer, attaching its eggs to the underside of the detrital debris in the bottom of the pools. Fatheads, both young and adult, in turn become food for orange-spotted and green sunfish and fish-eating birds and reptiles. Like the fathead, the black bullhead tolerates turbidity and poor water quality and feeds on some plant

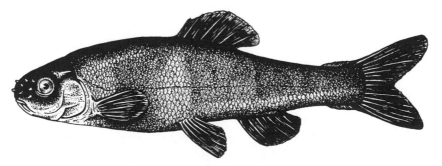

The fathead minnow survives in the murky, oxygen-bereft waters of prairie marshes and ephemeral streams.

material (although it depends largely on insect larvae) and finally becomes forage for other fish, reptiles, birds, and mammals. Thus a whole group of carnivorous animals exists upon those creatures that operate in the detritivore pathway. One of the most interesting of these is Graham's crayfish snake, which, as its name implies, feeds exclusively on the crayfish that scavenge plant and animal debris in the bottom of the marsh. This snake, in turn, is fed upon by herons, raccoons, and other snakes like the common kingsnake.

Crayfish, turtles, water snakes, and raccoons are the initial degraders of dead plant and animal material; carp and fathead minnows work over the bits and pieces of organic debris. The small invertebrates, however, wait to attack organic matter when its origins are unrecognizable. If you stand quietly in the marsh in some shaded spot where surface glare does not prevent you from peering closely into the water, you will discover a number of small creatures moving through the water above the bottom, some of them stopping from time to time to crawl about on submerged debris. These are the microcrustaceans, the cladocerans, copepods, and ostracods. These minute creatures filter out particulate organic matter or bacteria-encrusted clay particles as their source of food. They in turn become food for young carp and other small fish as well as for such avian predators as American avocets and northern shovelers.

Of these microcrustaceans, the ostracods are the most abundant at Cheyenne Bottoms. These wee creatures average only a millimeter in length and are like diminutive clams, their small bodies compressed between two chitinous shells held shut by a transverse muscle. They use their legs, which protrude from between the halves of their shell, to kick large pieces of debris into their mouths, or they sweep smaller particles from the water with long

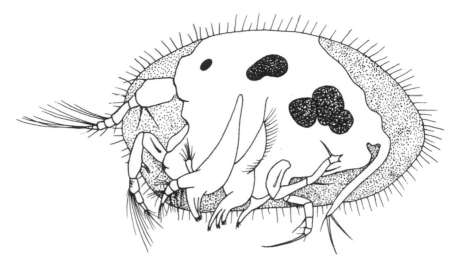

The most common "water flea" in the Bottoms is the ostracod, here with its left valve removed to reveal its body structure. Enlarged 85 times

bristles attached to their mouth parts. Still, the principal consumers of this particulate matter are the bloodworms, which in turn are preyed on by the carnivorous species of waterbirds that pass through the Bottoms in awesome abundance.

The huge biomass of bloodworms supports a large population of shorebirds. The shorebirds, in turn, support a few top carnivores. I remember that my eighth grade teacher at Bond Hill School in Cincinnati forbade the word "beautiful" when we wrote descriptions. Mrs. Firestone, I'm sorry; I do not know how else to succinctly summarize slowly driving along the dike at the Bottoms on an April morning and coming upon an adult male peregrine falcon in the middle of the road, feeding on a male yellow-headed blackbird, head feathers tinged with orange, the crimson drops of its blood contrasted against the shiny black of the plumage.

Blackbirds are the least dramatic prey of the majestic peregrine. The first peregrine I ever saw was coursing after shorebirds across the pools in the great Devonian coral reef that forms the Falls of the Ohio at Louisville, and these large falcons also come to the Bottoms in pursuit of migrant shorebirds. The presence of a peregrine over the marsh is signalled by the instantaneous rise of thousands of shorebirds into the air. Crossing above, in swift, purposeful flight, is the falcon. As the shorebirds twist and turn in tight, frantic flocks over the marsh, the peregrine crosses back, stooping down now at a particular flock, picking out a single bird that has separated from the tight mass. The straggler is pursued and sometimes caught in the falcon's claws as it sweeps past. Occasionally, at the very last moment, the shorebird veers out of reach, and the peregrine passes by empty-footed. Then the peregrine turns in a steep one-eighty, seeking out another potential prey, seldom getting a second chance at a near miss. If it does succeed in grasping a fleeing bird, the peregrine flies off to some perch to eat at leisure. Meanwhile the flocks of shorebirds pitch down to settle on the mudflats and feed again on bloodworms until the next pass of the peregrine startles them into flight, and again the sludge to blood-worm to sandpiper to peregrine pathway is played out in aerial maneuvers around the circle of the horizon.

Although blackbirds can be food for predaceous raptors, blackbirds are also predators themselves. The yellow-headed blackbird, for example, may feed on a newly-emerged dragonfly, which spent its early life underwater as a nymph feeding on bloodworms, mosquito larvae, snails, small fish, or anything else it could seize with a snap of its extendible lower lip. In due time the nymph climbs out of the water on a cattail stalk and is transformed into the darting adult, the devil's darning needle of childhood myth. For a short time during this metamorphosis, while its chitinous exoskeleton is hardening, it is especially vulnerable to predation. When I watched the

Hurtling down, a peregrine falcon selects its potential prey from among a frantic flock of shorebirds.

blackbird being eaten by the peregrine, I was seeing the last step in a food chain of four or five links. Such an unusual length emphasizes the richness of the detritivore-decomposer pathway.

Eventually all the organic matter produced in the marsh by the vegetation (matter which provides the foundation for the pyramid of consumers that live there) is broken down to simpler chemical forms. In a thin surface layer of soil under the water, chemical changes occur similar to those in terrestrial soils because of the availability of oxygen that is exchanged with the wind-ruffled water.

Here bacteria use organic compounds containing nitrogen, like proteins and nucleic acids, and the chitin derived from the exoskeletons of numerous invertebrates, converting them into ammonium, some of which diffuses into the water and the air as ammonia. Some ammonium diffuses directly into the roots of the marsh emergents to be used again in the manufacture of proteins; other molecules are oxidized by a set of different bacteria to produce nitrate. This more stable compound can enter into the roots of plants to be used again, or it can move down into the deeper anaerobic (oxygen-bereft) layers of the soil. The majority of the ammonium, however, is produced in the anaerobic zone of the soil where it binds to soil particles, enters into the plant root system, or diffuses up into the aerobic zone for further processing. The nitrates that move down into the anaerobic zone and are not absorbed by plants' roots are lost to the system as other bacteria convert nitrates into nitrous oxide and nitrogen gases, which then diffuse into the atmosphere from the soil and water.

Sulfur is an essential component in the proteins comprising the structures of plants and animals because it helps determine the three-dimensional shape of the molecules that prescribes their functions. This element is processed by the bacterial populations in both the aerobic and anaerobic zones of the submerged soil. In the aerobic zone sulfur is converted into sulfate, which can then be absorbed by the roots of plants for reuse. Under anaerobic conditions, sulfur is reduced to hydrogen sulfide, which then passes back into the atmosphere as a gas that smells like rotten eggs. Sulfides can also combine with iron in the soil to form ferrous sulfide, which gives the characteristic black coloration to the bottom muck.

Phosphorus is only a third as abundant in living tissue as nitrogen, but it plays an essential role in the metabolic transfer of energy in all living things. Factors affecting the eventual recycling of phosphorus are dependent on chemical events rather than on the activities of microbes. Phosphorus occurs as soluble compounds in combination with hydrogen and in this form can be taken up by the roots of plants for eventual incorporation into biologically important compounds. In the soil of the marsh phosphorus becomes unavailable to the biota when it is absorbed onto clay particles or precipitated in combination with iron, aluminum, and calcium under aerobic conditions.

To be used again by the biota, the carbon present in the organic compounds derived through the detritivore-decomposer pathway usually must be converted into the gas, carbon dioxide—although some compounds, like the simpler amino acids that comprise the building blocks of proteins, can be absorbed directly into the root system. Decomposition by bacteria in the presence of oxygen directly renders carbon dioxide. Under the anaerobic conditions prevailing in the submerged soils of the marsh, however, fermentation produces smaller, dissolved organic compounds, with or without the generation of some carbon dioxide. Certain bacterialike cells that are numbered among the most ancient forms of life on Earth, dating their origin to over 3.5 billion years ago, use organic compounds and even carbon dioxide under the reducing environment of the anaerobic zone to produce methane gas, which then escapes into the atmosphere. These methanogenic creatures are so different in their structure and physiology that they are considered by some biologists to belong in a unique kingdom, separate from other forms of life.

The roots of the emergent vegetation play an essential role as channels for the recycling of nutrients into the biotic phase of the ecosystem. These roots can function in the anaerobic environment of the submerged soil because of air spaces in their tissue. Almost 60 percent of the plant body is composed of these pore spaces which allow the diffusion of oxygen from the parts of the plant above water to those structures buried in the anaerobic muck. It had been generally accepted that this adaptation permitted root cells to carry on more efficient aerobic respiration, but recent research suggests that the gas volume available would support that level of metabolism for only a few hours. It is now hypothesized that the oxygen in these air spaces keeps roots functional by oxidizing metallic ions like iron that have precipitated on the surface of roots in a reduced form, impeding the role of the roots in nutrient uptake. The root cells of plants like cattails, adapted to growing in submerged soils, probably meet all their energy demands through anaerobic metabolic pathways.

EXPORTS AND IMPORTS IN THE MARSH ECONOMY

The majority of the marshes in the world carry on a lively commerce with other ecological systems. The salt marshes that border marine bays and estuaries are flushed seaward by the ebb of the tides and reflooded by the returning surge. Riverine marshes are continually washed by the downhill flow of the river. Materials processed by the detritivore-decomposer pathways in these marshes are exported through these currents. Rivers carry the eroded effluent of the land, providing imports to the marshes that border their channels as well as to the marshes in marine estuaries, and the returning tide brings additional imports to salt marshes. The marsh in Cheyenne Bottoms, however, is a relatively closed system. Imports are restricted, since extrinsic nourishment provided through the flows of Blood and Deception creeks is minimal. Outflow to the ground water is minuscule, and export through Little Cheyenne Creek occurs only during the rare periods of water overabundance. Thus, the carbon and nutrients fixed by the vegetation in the marsh that support both the herbivore-carnivore and detritivore-decomposer pathways stay in the marsh. That is almost the whole story, but not quite.

Like tourists from a cruise ship, the hordes of waterfowl and shorebirds that descend upon Cheyenne Bottoms during their migrations carry off products from the marsh. Using the population estimates of shorebirds during the spring migration of 1986, the approximations of the distances they still had to travel to reach their specific breeding grounds, and the published measurements of flight metabolism, Wayne Hoffman calculated that these birds carried away almost 2800 kilograms of fat stored within their bodies. To synthesize these fat stores the birds had to eat the equivalent of 150,000 kilograms of bloodworms. That's 165 tons of bloodworm protoplasm that would not be recycled in the marsh, although some of this material would be returned as metabolic waste products prior to the birds' departure. But the 3 tons of stored fat, of course, represents the minimum quantity of actual exports from the Bottoms.

Quantitative estimates of the effects of waterfowl on the economy of Cheyenne Bottoms are more difficult to calculate, since their diets are more variable and they spend considerable amounts of time feeding in fields outside of the marsh. In the fall of 1985, the peak population of ducks totaled about 80,000 birds; the peak for geese was 15,000. Wayne Hoffman calculated that these birds would require a little over 1900 tons of seeds to sustain this population during a 30-day layover period. His estimate did take into account that some of the waterfowl species have a diet that is only partly supplied by seeds. For example, only about half the food of the geese was seeds. The subset of this total seed ingestion that is the actual export term is not known. Nor is an estimate available for the vernal migratory period when reduced seed availability and the birds' physiological needs result in more carnivorous diets. But there is little doubt that waterfowl have an impact on the export of matter from Cheyenne Bottoms similar to that of the shorebirds.

In summer the large populations of red-winged blackbirds and yellow-headed blackbirds as well as the smaller numbers of common grackles and great-tailed grackles nesting in the marsh feed on a variety of emerging aquatic insects and caterpillars of the cattail moth. As consumers in both the herbivore-carnivore and detritivore-decomposer pathways within the marsh they are not greatly involved at this time in any import or export of materials, although when feeding nestlings they do make excursions to surrounding fields to gather terrestrial insects. After the breeding season, the numbers of blackbirds begin to increase as communal roosts develop, drawing upon blackbirds breeding in the adjacent countryside as well as migrants arriving from nesting areas elsewhere. An analysis of the returns of red-wings banded by Frank Robl, a longtime resident of Ellinwood, has shown that a majority of these migrants had bred in southern Saskatchewan. Most of the yellow-heads are gone by mid-November, and many of the red-wings migrate as well. Many of the birds banded by Robl wintered in Texas around Wichita Falls. But others remain, and by late February in 1986, for example, the roost totaled over half a million birds, composed of about 90 percent red-wings, followed in order of abundance by brown-headed cowbirds, European starlings, and common grackles. The birds roost in the cattails; in time, the stalks buckle under the sheer weight of the large numbers, and the roost shifts its location around the marsh.

The importance of the blackbirds as an avenue of im-

Blackbirds

port into the marsh economy during the nonbreeding season is substantial. Very few of the birds feed in the marsh
during the winter; rather, they forage all day on waste
grain in harvested fields, on standing grain sorghum
(milo), and on feed grains in cattle feedlots. But they come
back at dusk to roost in the marsh and to defecate, elimi-
nating indigestible materials as well as the waste products
of their metabolic processes, mostly nitrogen-containing
uric acid. Wayne Hoffman estimated the guano production of the roost during the winter of 1985–86 at 54 to 108

tons, which was largely derived from sources outside the marsh and hence provides a significant input of nitrogen. In the mid-1970s the roost was larger. Counts made at the roost during mid-winter in those years gave values of 9 to 12 million birds; thus, exogenous nitrogenous fertilization then might have been twenty times greater than the estimate for 1985–86.

5 Ecological Communities

At an altitude of 570 miles, Landsat circles the Earth in polar orbit. From this height the broad ecological patterns of North America are clearly visible through the wizardry of computer enhancement. The color in the eastern third of the continent is depicted as dark green, representing the verdant eastern deciduous forests. In the Great Plains the picture pales with the frequent interspersion of yellowish brown patches, denoting the westward trend of decreasing moisture under the lee of the snow-capped Rockies. Across the intermountain West, yellows and whites predominate, a reflection of aridity interrupted only by the north-south strips of green which highlight the folds in the earth's mantle thrust up to heights where they intercept Pacific moisture flowing across the land. And west of the Sierras the climatic reality of the "golden west" is apparent in the large areas of xeric yellows and tans. The Flint Hills and the High Plains of Kansas are clearly visible from this altitude, and the great bend of the Arkansas River is emphasized by the color separation of the sand prairie to its south and the mixed-grass prairie to its north. Just to the north of this arc of the Arkansas is the dark oval of Cheyenne Bottoms.

To describe patterns at the spatial scale of the communities where individual plants and animals actually live, we must come closer, down to a level where we can discern the interaction of the biota and the physical environment. An ecological community is an assemblage of plants and animals that live together in the same place and find their living requirements met by the physical variables in the environment and by other plants and animals occurring there. Within these ecological communities organisms participate in the processes of the ecosystem, the flow of energy and the cycling of matter. Ecological communities are typically named for the more overt, dominant plant species or general life-form of the plants present there. This is a shorthand reference that implies something about variables in the environment—whether it is multilayered like a forest or has the less vertical development of a grassland, whether it is wet like a marsh or dry like a prairie.

Attempts have been made to characterize communities in terms of a few habitat variables like the relative heterogeneity of the vegetation along horizontal and vertical axes, but such generalizations provide little predictive information about the discrete species of animals or the degree of plant and animal diversity that might be expected in that community. It is probably best, for the present, to attempt an understanding of the ecological community at a local level, a level that permits a more detailed investigation of the biotic and abiotic environment across both spatial and temporal dimensions. Unfortunately, there are very few of these kinds of studies, although the assessment study of Cheyenne Bottoms by the Kansas Biological Survey is at least a beginning.

THE UPLANDS: MIXED-GRASS PRAIRIE AND CROPLAND

As you approach the basin of the Bottoms from any direction except from Great Bend, you pass through an upland These prairies and most of the pastures are a mix of tall-

Grasses of the mixed-grass prairie: big bluestem, sideoats grama, and blue grama. Not to scale.

mosaic of tilled croplands, pastures, and native prairies. These prairies and most of the pastures are a mix of tall-grass species like big bluestem, mid-grasses like sideoats grama, and short grasses like blue grama and buffalo-grass. In an undisturbed state (that is, disturbed only by natural processes or by the best management practices which attempt to emulate natural disturbance), this community offers a dense layer of low-growing grasses and an upper, more open canopy of taller grasses and broad-leaved forbs. Like most grasslands throughout the world, the diversity of birds of the mixed-grass prairie is not great. There are western meadowlarks on the limestone fence posts in this land of few trees, grasshopper sparrows singing their monotone buzz from the tops of blue-stem clumps, a colony of dickcissels where the forbs are more dominant, ground-nesting mourning doves, and a few upland sandpipers. White-tailed deer browse in the early morning, and a coyote hurrying home to bed down before the heat of day stops to inspect a runway used by the abundant prairie vole. Plains garter snakes and bull-snakes are also relatively common predators of the mixed-grass prairie, sharing many prey species with the coyotes.

At several locations in grazed prairies and pastures, some within the basin of Cheyenne Bottoms, black-tailed prairie dogs have established their societies, clearing the vegetation from the hillocks of their burrows so that their view of the world is not obscured. Ferrets are not to be expected, but the approach of other predators like coyotes demands continual surveillance. The swift passage of a prairie falcon down from the Front Range in autumn, however, gives little time for warning; and ferruginous hawks congregate at the dogtowns to catch these nonhi-bernating rodents as they come out to investigate the winter day. The insectivorous burrowing owl, which does not

The prairie grasses offer abundant sustenance, but life in the middle of the food web demands constant vigilance by the black-tailed prairie dog.

burrow, uses old dog burrows for its own reproductive purposes, and the dogtowns around the Bottoms usually harbor a few owls.

Another mammal that can be found in more open grasslands is the black-tailed jack rabbit, but it is not common. Where grass is denser and woody vegetation like shelterbelts provides additional cover, the more abundant eastern cottontail bolts from underfoot. Badgers prefer open prairies and pastures as well, but are uncommon in this vicinity, probably because prey species like pocket gophers are also uncommon. The bison are gone, but flocks of brown-headed cowbirds now follow cattle, catching insects put to flight by their grazing, a cooperative arrangement also enjoyed by cattle egrets.

In these uplands adjacent to the Bottoms certain "shorebirds" are to be expected during their periods of passage. Occasionally found on the mudflats in the marsh, the lesser golden plover, a species that nests in grassy tundra, also forages in grazed pastures. This is also true of the less frequently seen buff-breasted sandpiper, which also nests in drier grassy tundra, and the long-billed curlew, a species that breeds on the short-grass prairie of the High Plains.

The patches of croplands are monocultures that offer little biotic diversity because of the uniformity of their structure and because the husbandry employed mechanically and chemically eliminates the competition and interdicts energy flow by reducing the herbivorous insects. During the late spring and early summer, however, the horned lark finds this a good nesting habitat if it is fortunate enough to elude the harrow, and the "short-grass prairie" of winter wheat attracts thousands of lapland longspurs that come down from the arctic tundra in November. When left as summer fallow, croplands attract a broader biota—herbivorous rodents like voles, deer mice, and ground squirrels, and insectivorous birds like dickcissels and red-winged blackbirds.

WHEATGRASS/SALTGRASS COMMUNITY

The ecological communities in the Bottoms are distributed according to the availability of water. Prior to the construction of the dikes that divided the area into separate pools, the communities were arrayed much like an archery target, with open water at the bull's eye and the other communities forming more or less concentric, broad circles around the central pool, ordered outward by increasing tolerance to decreasing soil water. Building the dikes separated centers of open water with their associated water-dependent communities, but the most arid community, the wheatgrass/saltgrass association, still remains at the higher elevations around the periphery of the basin. These two dominants are not intermingled, since wheatgrass occurs on drier soils and saltgrass prefers more mesic sites, but the spatial distribution varies in relation to the conditions of the rainfall-dependent soil moisture at the Bottoms. The broad-leaved forbs occurring in this community present a spring aspect of yarrow, prickly poppy, wild licorice, and hemp dogbane, and a summer aspect of wooly vervain, silver-leaf nightshade, western ragweed, and curlycup gumweed. Additionally, annual brome, foxtail barley, and inland rush are noticeable monocots. Within the last 20 years, willow baccharis and salt cedar (tamarisk) have invaded. The latter species is considered especially noxious because its long root system taps deep soil water, increasing evapotranspiration loss. In shallow depressions scattered across these flats where standing water has repeatedly evaporated, increasing the salt concentration in the soil, stands of saltbush, spearscale, sea blite, and plains bluegrass develop in late summer.

The animals associated with this community are those of the mixed-grass prairie, the species responding more to the life forms of the plants rather than to the kinds of plants. The proximity to the marsh results in many duck species—mallards, shovelers, and teal—building their nests here. Within small areas of saltgrass that are wet in the spring so that rushes, sedges, wild licorice, and Illinois bundleflower can grow, eastern meadowlarks rather than western meadowlarks occur along with dickcissels, grasshopper sparrows, and red-winged blackbirds. Bobolinks sometimes arrive to nest in years when these patches are truly wet meadows, forming a disjunct population of these handsome blackbirds far to the south of the main nesting range that extends across the Dakotas east to the lake states. In years of especially abundant water when this habitat actually floods, soras have been found nesting, even as late as early August.

Wheatgrass and saltgrass. Not to scale.

SPIKESEDGE COMMUNITY

A little over half a century ago when Uhler and Warren made the earliest vegetation survey of Cheyenne Bottoms, spikesedge formed an almost uniform band between the open water/bulrush and the wheatgrass/saltgrass communities. At the present time, however, spikesedge is scattered within the wheatgrass/saltgrass flats where small depressions 6 to 12 inches deep provide standing water into late spring in most years. This persistence of water is enough to prevent the invasion of saltgrass, permitting the development of a distinctly different association of plants. Spikesedge begins to grow in late March, blooms, and sets fruit before summer arrives. As the water dries down, dock and ironweed develop to dominate the summer aspect. Other important plant species in this community are foxtail grasses and barnyard grass, a wild relative of domesticated millet.

During migration, this community is the preferred habitat of both the lesser and greater yellowlegs and the pectoral sandpiper, but common snipe, willets, various "peeps," Wilson's phalaropes, and American avocets can be seen as well. Sometimes long-billed curlew feed here alongside white-faced ibis and various herons. The only nesting records for black rails in the Bottoms were reported in this habitat, and Wilson's phalaropes also select this area for breeding, the pale males assuming the incubation duties and early care of the young while the brightly feathered females enjoy emancipation from domestic chores. Snowy plovers nest on the barren, saline soil adjacent to sedge pools. This is certainly the best habitat for seeing American bitterns while they search the shallows and water margins, feeding on small mammals, snakes, and frogs.

CATTAIL COMMUNITY

The cattails have existed in the Bottoms at least since the Pleistocene, but within the last quarter century their presence and impact in the marsh have changed from insignificant to dominant. This transformation has resulted largely from the invasion of the narrow-leaved cattail into the region, although the broad-leaved cattail still remains. Growth begins in mid-March; by mid-June the cattails at Cheyenne Bottoms are producing the familiar cylindrical spike of dense flowers. Cattails remain physiologically active until the first frost, unless they are either flooded or killed by extended drought. The narrow-leaved cattail appears to be better adapted than the broad-leaved cattail to fluctuating water levels and has a greater tolerance to salinity, conditions that characterize Cheyenne Bottoms. Furthermore, the narrow-leaved cattail is a highly effective converter of solar radiation into plant biomass.

Cattails form a broad band of vegetation around the margins of the pools in water depths of two feet or less, but they are unable to survive in deeper water. In shallower pools they form dense stands that completely exclude open water and cover exposed ground that otherwise might be used by aquatic wildlife for feeding and loafing. This increase in cattails has been accompanied by a decrease in coverage by bulrush, which once spread across large areas; the bulrush, along with arrowhead in shallow sites, provided a greater diversity of plant life. Rushes now grow confined to zones scattered within the cattails or as islands in the pools beyond the rim of cattails.

While the biomass of bloodworms in cattails is less than 5 percent of that in submerged mud, it is still substantial. The greatest diversity of invertebrate animals is associated with the cattail community, especially along the edge of the cattails where these plants interface with open water. Here the median diversity value for the six monthly samples taken during the assessment study is almost twice as large as that for the submerged mud community. The next highest values of species richness were shared by the samples collected in emergent mixed forbs (e.g., pigweed, kochia), Japanese millet, and the interior of the cattail stands. Because it is the main avenue for the input of energy into the marsh, the cattail community can naturally support such a large complement of organisms that are participating primarily in the detritivore-decomposer pathway.

Much of what goes on in the cattail community is obscured by the curtain of densely packed leaves. You share the frustration of Kipling's Ethiopian after the leopard moved to other spots; you can hear sounds of life and perhaps even smell life, but you cannot see life. Coots cackle and croak, bitterns pump, bullfrogs groan, pied-billed grebes sound like misplaced cuckoos, mysterious splashes are accompanied by suggestive partings of leaves, soras whinny, Virginia rails grunt, carp thrash about, and still you see nothing. The marsh is indeed a "haunt of coot and her'n."

The only way to know the cattail community is to enter and merge yourself with the marsh. But for very good reasons related to the welfare of the inhabitants, this is not permitted at Cheyenne Bottoms. For several summers during my college years in Michigan I worked as a nature counselor in a children's camp. Occasionally on my once-a-week day off I had to go to Detroit to be reassured that civilization was still extant (I'm not sure that goal would be attained in these latter days). But my best days off were spent in a small glacial marsh just down the Dryden road, where I could stand hidden in the vegetation, immersed thigh deep in the water. Marsh wrens rattled above my head, least bitterns braced their legs akimbo between the stalks of the cattails while they hunted, young zebra-striped grebes rode the backs of their parents, diving beetles hurried past with bright red mites inserted in the sutures of their exoskeletons, turtles swam by to raise their snouts above the water almost at my fingertips, and leeches measured my trouser leg, searching for entry. Close up, a marsh is a joy.

Personnel on official business have been able to explore the cattail community at Cheyenne Bottoms so that we can appreciate something of what is going on in there. The three most abundant fish species are the fathead minnow, the black bullhead, and the common carp. The only other fishes in this community are the predaceous green and orange-spotted sunfishes. The diversity is low because conditions of turbidity, temperature, and oxygen concentration are harsh, but all of these species are links in the detritivore-decomposer food web. Painted turtles float along the edge of the cattails, the dark triangles of their beaks protruding across the surface of the water, snorkels for exchanging respiratory gases. Others bask on debris only to slide shyly under the water when you approach. Less commonly found are the slider and the yellow mud turtle; both find the mud bottoms of the marsh to their liking. Out of sight, the ubiquitous snapping turtle lurks in the depths, growing big on abundant prey. When the marsh is sucked dry by prolonged drought, the snapping turtle must move to find water, but the yellow mud turtle burrows in the bottom muck until good times return. The diamond-backed water snake is seen most frequently swimming through the water but can be found in full view if you inspect the tops of muskrat houses or walk along the water's edge. Bullfrogs and the plains leopard frogs occur but are susceptible to interruption of their life cycle by periodic drought, and hence their numbers fluctuate considerably. The mink and its muskrat prey are the mammals of the cattail community, but striped skunks, raccoons, and opossums forage in the marsh, especially when nestling birds are available.

The advent of the extensive cattail community has resulted in an increased diversity of the breeding bird population at Cheyenne Bottoms. Although white-faced ibis bred at the Bottoms in bulrushes as early as 1951, the large colony of herons did not develop until after the cattails had become well established in the early 1970s, probably a result of the greater structural support provided by their stout stems. Guy Ernsting's study of heron colonies in Kansas, as well as reports by Schwilling and Zuvanich, has documented the species composition of the colonies during several years of observations. Black-crowned night-herons are always the most abundant, numbering in the hundreds, but the populations of the other species—cattle egret, snowy egret, little blue heron, white-faced ibis, and yellow-crowned night-heron—vary in order of abundance. All of these herons nest above the surface of the water, but the night-herons' nests are placed deep within the cattails, and the other species' nests are several feet above the water. One year, an extralimital tricolored heron joined the colony, but subsequent drying of the marsh allowed raccoons to enter and plunder the nest before its young could fledge. Since then, however, tricolors have bred here successfully.

Of these species, only the night-herons and, to a lesser extent, the snowy egrets do most of their feeding in the marsh. Black-crowned night-herons have even been observed actually swimming in pursuit of fish. Cattle egrets, natural immigrants that finally reached Kansas from African savannas in the early 1960s, maintain their commensal relationships with large herbivores in the absence of wildebeests and zebra by joining cattle in the pastures to feed on the insects flushed by their grazing. Little blue herons and ibis also can be found frequently feeding in upland grasslands, but they rely upon their own efforts to secure bugs. Least bitterns nest in solitude on platforms built well above the water in the cattails. American bitterns, in contrast, usually select terrestrial nest sites in tall grasses adjacent to the marsh.

The heron colonies are surrounded by nesting yellow-headed blackbirds. In the spring red-winged blackbirds arrive early and establish territories throughout the marsh, but the larger-bodied yellow-heads, coming later, easily usurp the space from the red-wings in these central areas. The red-wings are pushed aside, maintaining their territories around the periphery of the cluster of yellow-head territories. These territories may reflect the yellow-heads' preference for deeper water, which certainly makes the nests less vulnerable to mammalian predators as the drydown of summer contracts the water surface, but Gordon Orians suggests that the location may also reflect an avoidance of the edge where trees occur along the dikes. Red-wings do not mind trees; in fact, they display in the trees and also forage in them. Yellow-heads, however, put considerable distance between their nests and the bordering trees and prefer open fields outside the marsh for their foraging excursions. In early May of 1989, the marsh was dry and yellow-heads did not nest in the cattails, but the less finicky red-wings did. Deep water thus appears to be an important variable in breeding site selection for yellow-headed blackbirds.

The great-tailed grackle arrived in the vicinity of the Bottoms in 1969, after irrupting across the Red River into Oklahoma from central Texas less than a decade before. By 1974 numerous great-tailed females had formed a nesting cluster in the cattails around the heron colony and have continued to breed in the marsh. The strikingly different males can be regularly observed at display sites in uplands around the basin where their loud clear whistles and percussive clackings attract females for brief, promiscuous liaisons.

Most of the common breeding ducks that frequent the marsh do not nest in the cattail community but choose dry sites in the surrounding uplands where clumps of tall grass and shrubs provide sufficient cover. The redheads and ruddy ducks, however, both build their nests in clumps of cattails or bulrushes, though slightly above the water. American coots, common moorhens, and Virginia rails also build their nests over water, and pied-billed grebes, Forster's terns, and black terns build floating nests in patches of open water within the cattails, sometimes using each other's old platforms. Although the terns have not been observed using muskrat lodges at Cheyenne Bottoms, Canada geese do use these piles as nesting platforms.

OPEN-WATER/MUDFLAT COMMUNITIES

It is a rare day when the wind does not blow across Cheyenne Bottoms. Because of the wind, submerged vegetation is sparce; the wind-driven waves tear at the bottom of the pools, preventing successful rooting and throwing the bottom silts up into the water, making photosynthesis marginal in the resulting turbidity. The Mosaic miracle of the Red Sea is repeated in miniature almost daily at the Bottoms as the prevailing wind piles water on the leeward sides of the pools, exposing miles of mudflats that are reflooded when the wind moderates or shifts in its direction. Except for the deeper regions of the pools, what is mudflat and what is open water is a function of wind direction and velocity.

American avocets and snowy plovers nest on the barren, exposed mudflats. For over 80 percent of the shorebird species and almost a third of the waterfowl species, open water and mudflats are the feeding habitats of primary preference. Add in the grebes, cormorants and white pelicans, gulls and terns, cranes, coots, great blue herons, ospreys, and bald eagles, and you get a diversity of colors, shapes, sizes, feeding styles, and patterns of activity that delights the spirit and exemplifies what the concern for the Bottoms is all about. Not only is this habitat essential to the continued biological welfare of the species that sustain their lives here, but also for an increasingly large number of people, experiencing this habitat is essential for sustaining their humanity.

As the water continues to evaporate, by late June and early July during average years annual plants invade the drying mud. Kochia and saltmarsh aster are the two most common, forming dense stands, but Russian thistle, snow-on-the-mountain, goosefoot, pigweed, sprangletop, and barnyard grass grow up, flower, and set seeds. Damper depressions are invaded by annual smartweeds and water hemp. These mud flats are also purposely seeded to Japanese millet and wheat to increase food for waterfowl by the time of their autumnal arrival when water should be available to reflood the vegetated flats. White-fronted geese are especially attracted then, but blue-winged teal, American wigeon, and northern pintail also prefer this habitat.

DIKE COMMUNITY

The dikes, of course, have been at the Bottoms only since the development of the refuge in the early 1950s, but about one-half of the plant species known for this site have occurred on these drier, unnatural ridges that border the marsh. Cottonwood, green ash, the poisonous water hemlock, smartweed, cocklebur, sunflower, pigweed, and

With expanded throat and hunched wings to display his scarlet epaulets, the male red-winged blackbird sings to maintain his territory among the cattails, ensuring his exclusive access to his several mates.

wild lettuce do provide cover, support insects, and produce seeds that benefit a variety of animal species, either directly as herbivores or insectivores, or as carnivores like the massasauga rattler and racerunner. Killdeers nest on the dikes, and hundreds of swallows gather along the dikes to feed on the swarms of midges performing their mating dance over the roads.

6   Shorebird Patterns of Passage

Fossil evidence for the presence of shorebirds in the rapidly unfolding phylogenetic radiation of birds after their derivation from the archosaurian reptiles goes back to the late Cretaceous, around 80 million years ago. Although shorebirds have been around a long time, the huge numbers that we enjoy must be a phenomenon manifest only since the Pleistocene. Shorebirds occur throughout the world, breeding on all continents and in all biomes, but it is the Holarctic tundra that sustains the reproduction of the most species and generates the densities that we see as they pass through temperate zone staging areas. Arctic tundra nesting species that are common during migration at Cheyenne Bottoms are black-bellied plover, lesser golden plover, semipalmated plover, Hudsonian godwit, semipalmated sandpiper, western sandpiper, least sandpiper, white-rumped sandpiper, Baird's sandpiper, pectoral sandpiper, stilt sandpiper, and long-billed dowitcher.

The tundra has existed as an integrated ecological system in its present circumpolar distribution, however, only during interglacial periods. These arctic-breeding shorebird populations must have been drastically reduced during the periods of glacial advance when suitable habitat was compressed into the various ice-free refugia, since there is no evidence for a broad skirt of tundra along the advancing or retreating ice. Subarctic muskeg breeders common at the Bottoms are the greater and lesser yellow-legs. Although patches of muskeg probably occurred throughout the band of boreal forest abutting the edge of the glaciers, the range of this biome was smaller during periods of maximum glacial advance than it is today, and these sandpipers would have been probably less abundant also.

The days are long at high latitudes as shorebirds arrive to take advantage of an environment where few other kinds of birds compete for the abundant insect food in the shallow pools and their bordering gardens of mosses, lichens, dwarf willows, and wildflowers which form above the permafrost during the June thaw; but the season is short. Intraspecific competition, of course, is intense, and most species are territorial, sequestering the resources necessary for their success. This behavior actually reduces the hassle of prolonged aggressive interactions, increases the probability of mating, and permits devotion to the critical behaviors associated with reproduction. Daylight is just about continuous, providing long hours for feeding on bountiful resources when the young hatch so that they grow and develop rapidly. Adult mortality rates on the breeding grounds are low and the annual survival rates high, seventy percent or greater, about twice as high as that of temperate-breeding passerines. But the shorebirds usually get only one chance at reproduction; if spring is late, they may not breed at all that year.

Adults of most species depart their arctic breeding ranges to begin the migration south during July and August, leaving their precocial young to fend for themselves. After acquiring the prerequisite fat stores, which need not be excessively large for the first leg south, the young of the year set off alone to begin their virginal migration a couple of weeks later. The adults initiate molting before leaving, but this energy-consuming process is arrested prior to their departure and resumes later on the winter range. In their haste to evade the imminent polar winter, juveniles either postpone the molt completely until after migration or attenuate the process so that their energy income can be optimally budgeted toward the demands of flight.

It seems as if the birds leave when the habitat is lavish. But the climate changes rapidly after the summer solstice; the birds must match the timing of their itinerary with the suitability of the habitats in the chain of critical stopover sites that sustain their largely transequatorial migration in order to arrive propitiously in the austral spring. They fly fast, 50 to 80 kilometers per hour; and they fly high, frequently at altitudes above 10,000 feet. Apparently, the advantage of flight in the colder air at high altitudes is primarily to facilitate heat loss, since the energy demanded by their sustained muscular effort is enormous and the elimination of heat is a problem with which they must contend. Indeed, dehydration due to the evaporation of water from the breathing system, which prevents dangerously elevated body temperatures, is more limiting for all migrant birds than the quantity of energy in fat stores.

Little is known about the navigational abilities of the various shorebird species, although Franz Sauer demonstrated over a quarter century ago that lesser golden plovers use celestial cues to provide a means of orientation that takes them along the proper migratory routes. Until contrary evidence is provided, I assume that the navigational system of shorebirds is similar to that of passerines, like buntings, Old World warblers, and starlings, about which we know much more. After mid-June the photoperiod rapidly shortens. At 70 degrees north, about the middle of many species' breeding ranges, daylength has dropped close to 18 hours by the time the young are ready to move south in mid-August. The young birds must learn the position of north as the images of the stars rotating around the celestial pole during the short arctic night cross the visual receptors in their retinas, but the correct azimuth to fly in response to the patterns in the night sky is programmed into their genetic material. Whether this orientation takes them in the proper direction of south or north is dependent on the daily secretions of hormones, prolactin from the anterior pituitary and glucocorticoids from the adrenal gland, whose releases are regulated by a circadian cycle that has evolved to accommodate the rapidly retreating hour of dawn. Perhaps when the birds have flown beyond the confusing convergence of the lines of flux in the Earth's magnetic field at higher latitudes, they can use geomagnetism for orientation when the ice crystals in the high cirrus obscure the night sky. Stopover sites are traditional, and young birds fix the latitude and longitude (or whatever unknown bicoordinate system the birds use) in their central nervous systems so that in subsequent years their path can be more easily corrected for displacement resulting from unexpected crosswinds.

We don't have warbler waves on the prairie, but migration does not pass by unrecognized. Swirling columns of Franklin's gulls catch insects uplifted in the thermals. The falsetto honks of white-fronted geese descend from the dark on an October morning, but it is the soft, twittering calls of upland sandpipers spaced across the range of my hearing in the sky of a September night that produce the shivers of Wanderlust for me. A sign on the interstate just this side of Topeka advertised, "Salina tonight, the Rockies tomorrow." The upland sandpipers reassure one another as they pass on quivering wings in the dark above my head, "the Flint Hills tonight, the pampas by the weekend."

Each shorebird species passing through Cheyenne

Against the rising spring moon, shorebirds depart the Bottoms, driven by innate mechanisms evolving through the experiences of generations.

Bottoms has its own species-specific migratory pattern, but two generalized groupings can be made: semiannual and loop migrations. Transit through the Great Plains in the spring and the fall is the most common pattern, for both arctic and temperate-breeding species. Some of the species in this group also migrate along either the Pacific or the Atlantic coasts, or both. Other species cross the Great Plains only once, in either the spring or the fall, using coastal routes for the other limb of their elliptical journeys.

SEMIANNUAL MIGRANTS

The breeding range of the Baird's sandpiper is almost completely above the Arctic Circle. Adults are already on the move by late June and early July, the females starting ahead of the males. They track a narrow path through the central Great Plains, flying over Alberta and Manitoba to alight in eastern Colorado, Kansas, Oklahoma, and west Texas. The juveniles come later, after the middle of August, and are spread across a much wider swath of the North American continent, many regularly moving east to the Atlantic coast where their scaly-backed plumage has been institutionalized in field guides as the norm for the species. Traveling more slowly than the adults, they tarry here and there but eventually work their way southwest to Texas and Arizona. The first adults appear at Cheyenne Bottoms during the second week of July and become increasingly more numerous by the last week, peaking during the first two weeks of August but remaining abundant until the first week in September.

The Bottoms is a critical juncture in the migratory pathways of the species, and the dilemma created by its being completely dry when they arrive has dismal ramifications. From this staging area, and others less well known west throughout the High Plains, the birds will depart with a following wind after cold front passage on a direct, nonstop flight of around 4,000 miles to the Andes in northern South America. The juveniles make a similar leap from the southwest. Records are few for Mexico and Middle America; it is probable that the birds fly a great circle route over water off the Pacific coast to landfall in Peru. They move still farther south along the cordillera from Ecuador and central Peru all the way to Tierra del Fuego to winter on interior wetlands and grasslands. The return flight to the arctic retraces the fall passage, with the species being most numerous at the Bottoms from the end of March to the middle of May. From there they probably make a single nonstop flight to the tundra in time to mesh their reproductive cycle with the awakening of the brief arctic summer.

The semipalmated sandpiper migrates broadly across the plains. Banding records and their smaller body size indicate that the semipalmated sandpipers passing through Cheyenne Bottoms in the fall come from the western Arctic of North America and eastern Asia, where they nest in wet tundra or on the water-logged islands of lakes, rivers, and ponds. The passage south begins early; adult females precede the males, and only the juveniles remain on the tundra by the middle of August. The species moves through the Great Plains east of the Rocky Mountains, arriving at the Bottoms in large numbers by the third week of July and remaining at peak numbers until mid-September. Perhaps the concentrations at staging areas like Cheyenne Bottoms in the interior of the continent are not as spectacular as they are on the upper reaches of the Bay of Fundy because the subsequent movement south involves only a trans-Gulf leap to the coast of Venezuela, whereas the birds on the Atlantic Coast must gain sufficient fat for a 50- to 60-hour flight over water to South America.

Once in northern South America a few birds move west to winter on the Pacific coast of Peru, but the majority fly east to the coast of Surinam where they constitute about 70 percent of the approximately 2 million birds that winter on the mudbanks there. This important shoal of fertile, crustacean-rich mud has arisen from silt carried down from the Andes in the Amazon drainage and transported coastwise by the Guiana current northwest to Surinam. Although some of the birds go farther south to the coast of Brazil, semipalmated sandpipers do not migrate as far as the Baird's and white-rumps. In the fine-tuned evolution of avian morphologies, the longer, distance-adapted wings of these latter two species extend beyond the tail when they are furled along the back, giving their bodies a diagnostic tear-drop shape. The tips of the semi-palmated sandpiper's wings, on the other hand, lie even with the end of its tail, making its posterior appear truncated. The return trip to the western arctic retraces the fall path; individuals banded in the spring at Cheyenne Bottoms have been recaptured in the same pools during the following fall. Many individuals, however, who had taken the Atlantic route in the fall also appear at the Bottoms, choosing to return north through the plains.

Other arctic-nesting species have similar migratory routes that connect with south temperate winter ranges. Stilt and pectoral sandpipers move broadly through the plains in both the spring and the fall. Even pectoral sandpipers breeding in central Siberia fly east to the western hemisphere, apparently retracing the history of past range expansions, before turning south toward the winter range in nonmaritime regions of South America. During the spring both these species are most common at the Bottoms throughout May and in the fall become abundant in late July and early August. Stilt sandpiper numbers begin to wane in mid-September, but pectorals are still coming through in large numbers until the middle of October. The least sandpiper uses both coasts in addition to the Great Plains during its periods of passage and is most numerous at the Bottoms from late April to mid-May and again from mid-July to the first week in November. Semipalmated plovers have a similar migratory pattern, peaking in abundance at the Bottoms from the last week in April through the first week in May and from early August to mid-September during the trip south. Long-billed dowitchers migrate through the plains west to the Pacific shore and are most numerous at the Bottoms throughout April to mid-May and from late July to the first week in November. Black-bellied plovers are primarily coastal migrants, but a few regularly use an interior route and are most numerous at the Bottoms throughout May and from late August to early October during the period of their passage south.

Both the lesser and greater yellowlegs move broadly from their subarctic nesting grounds in the muskeg to reach their wintering ranges which extend all the way from the Gulf coast to Tierra del Fuego. In the spring, the greater yellowlegs become numerous in late March, but the numbers of the lesser yellowlegs do not substantially increase at the Bottoms until the last week in April. Both species are seen less frequently after mid-May but then become common again from mid-July to late September and early October.

The locally breeding American avocet remains abundant at the Bottoms from mid-April to mid-October and follows a migratory route through the interior of North America to and from a winter range stretching from the Gulf coast to Middle America. The marbled godwit nests farther north in the prairie pothole region and passes through the Bottoms in large numbers during late April and again from late July to early September on its way to winter along the coasts of the United States to northern South America. The willet, which breeds across a wider temperate range than the godwit, has a pattern of migration and phenology through the Bottoms similar to that of the semipalmated plover. The Wilson's phalarope is present at Cheyenne Bottoms from mid-April to early September with nesting occurring from late May to early July. The species nests throughout the northern grasslands and migrates south through western North America, staging in large numbers at Mono Lake in California and wintering in western South America on lakes in the Andes Mountains from Peru to Argentina.

LOOP MIGRANTS

The white-rumped sandpiper is similar in size and shape to the Baird's sandpiper and is sympatric with the Baird's in the central part of the latter's arctic breeding range. In all other aspects of their natural histories they are quite different. The white-rumps select breeding sites in wetter habitats along the borders of streams and ponds, whereas the Baird's chooses inland limestone flats, bleak hills, and dry, upland plateaus. Unlike the monogamous Baird's (the males share in the attentive duties to the clutch), the white-rumps have a polygynous mating system and the males take no part in incubation, withdrawing to the beaches in mid-summer. After the young hatch, the females join the males in early August. Having completed their physiological premigratory preparation, the males leave first, but the females follow soon after. Like the Baird's, the juvenile white-rumps leave last; but the species lingers in the north longer than the Baird's, not completely disappearing from the breeding range until late October.

There are few fall records for the sandpipers at Cheyenne Bottoms, since initially most of the white-rumps fly east to the Atlantic seaboard along Labrador, Nova Scotia, and the coast of New Brunswick. From there they make a direct flight to Surinam, passing through in late August and September, cross Amazonia to the Rio Grande do Sul in Brazil, and track down to Cape Horn and Tierra del Fuego. Although there is some overlap in the wintering range between the two species, the white-rumps remain primarily in the Atlantic littoral while the Baird's occurs west toward the mountains. The return flight follows a different route north through Venezuela and to the Great Plains of North America, with the white-rumps becoming abundant at Cheyenne Bottoms from mid-May to early June, well after the peak migration of the Baird's has passed. It is hypothesized that this migratory pattern has evolved in this species and the other eastern loop migrants because the coast of the maritime provinces of Canada from which they depart in the fall is too recently released from the grip of winter to provide the necessary nourishment; the plains provide a more sanguine habitat at a time necessary to ensure a seasonal arrival on the breeding range. From the Bottoms, the white-rumps make a single, nonstop flight to the tundra, completing their circuitous migratory path.

For many years the Hudsonian godwit was an enigma to provincial eastern ornithologists because so few were ever seen. Indeed, it was considered close to extinction. Further field efforts revealed, however, that it arrives by the thousands during late July and early August at James Bay from its disjunct breeding grounds along the coast of the Beaufort Sea and Hudson Bay. From James Bay the godwits apparently make a direct flight of around 3,000 miles to South America, although there are an adult and juvenile in the museum at the University of Kansas, collected at the Bottoms during September. The godwits' migration is not well documented until they arrive on their winter range in Argentina, but by the middle of the austral summer they are abundant along the coastline in Patagonia and Tierra del Fuego. Like white-rumped sandpipers, Hudsonian godwits return north through the Great Plains and are most numerous at Cheyenne Bottoms from late April to late May. Most of the birds return to the low Arctic during the first week of June.

Probably the best known loop migrant is the lesser

golden plover. Adults leave the high Arctic beginning in August, but the young of the year depart in September, moving southeast around both coasts of Hudson Bay to the maritime provinces of Canada and the northeastern states. From there they cross the ocean directly to South America, where they winter in both coastal and interior grassland habitats from Bolivia to northern Argentina. Migration north through the Great Plains brings them to Cheyenne Bottoms in the largest numbers during the middle fortnight of May. Unlike with the previous two species, there are enough fall records at the Bottoms, including several hundred birds seen by Chuck Ely in October, to suggest that some plovers choose the interior route for both seasons of passage.

Western sandpipers migrate the other way around and are abundant at the Bottoms from the middle of July to the third week of September and irregular and uncommon in the spring. Only a portion of the species population, however, makes this loop by coasting along the Gulf of Alaska and ranging more easterly at the Frasier River delta to join others coming directly inland from the North Slope. Banding returns reveal that the birds passing through Cheyenne Bottoms then continue southeast to Florida, the Yucatan Peninsula, and Guyana. Most of the species, on the other hand, leave the tundra breeding grounds—on islands in the Bering Sea and along the coasts of northwestern Alaska and the Chukchi Peninsula in Siberia—and migrate down the Pacific coast of North America, filling the intertidal with flocks of "peeps" much as the semipalmated sandpipers populate the eastern littoral. From there they continue south along the Pacific coast to northern Peru, although some fly east to join the semipalms along the Atlantic coast of Surinam. Almost the entire population follows the Pacific shore for the return to the tundra.

Cheyenne Bottoms provides the nexus for the path-

Hudsonian godwits

ways of tens of thousands of shorebirds, some numerous and others very rare. I suspect that the last of the Eskimo curlews still makes a furtive visit as it flies its lonely path between the plains of Patagonia and the Mackenzie valley. Yet the abundant Baird's, white-rumps, dowitchers, and stilt sandpipers face impending adversity as humankind preempts the water that supports this wetland. The shorebirds have evolved a whole suite of adaptations in the expectation that the world would continue to be fruitful. Their struggle for existence is predicated on the perpetual variability in the genetic composition of individuals that arises through the recombinations offered by the sexual reproduction of every generation; thus, modifications in the birds' morphological, physiological, and behavioral characteristics could anticipate environmental shifts and progress at rates commensurate with the intensity of environmental change. The shorebirds, however, are dependent on a critical bottleneck in their annual cycle that is in danger of occlusion because Cheyenne Bottoms has problems. The rate of decline in the Bottoms' suitability may exceed the adaptation rate of the species dependent on this habitat.

The problem with the Bottoms, however, is not unique; it is a microcosm of the environmental crisis confronting the entire planet. The grace by which the Earth was created and sustained must compete with an aggressive avarice that served us well as we emerged beyond the African veld a long, long time ago and spread across the full expanse of the globe. Now this materialism, exaggerated in the developed countries but barely providing subsistence in the developing nations, threatens the integrity of the biosphere. Who shall inherit the Earth? Who, indeed!

7 The Problem

The water transfer system at Cheyenne Bottoms was designed to depend on gravity flow through concrete channels between the pools that could be used selectively by opening or closing the gated outlets. The bottom elevation of these channels was chosen to equal that of the barrow ditches along the dikes and into which these outlets open. This level, of course, was below that of the pools. Since water runs downhill and whatever is in the water goes along with the flow, these low places became the sites of silt deposition. Thus the approaches to the gated channels became partially blocked, greatly reducing the ability to transfer water between the pools. Furthermore, the barrow ditches themselves have filled with silt and can no longer function to drain the pools. The pumping station on the dike between two peripheral pools transfers water into the central pool but cannot operate continuously at full capacity because the rate of drainage from these perimeter pools is too slow to keep up with the pumps, and the inlet channel becomes dry. The freedom to respond rapidly to changes in the water levels of the various pools and to transfer water into the central storage pool has been drastically curtailed by inadequacies in the initial design but especially by the very fact that the area is topographically the Bottoms.

The rate of water loss by evaporation is proportional

to the exposed surface area. The central pool covers 3,300 acres. In dry periods this pool is too large to fill, resulting in a broad expanse of shallow water, ideal for maximum evaporative loss. The peripheral pools have a similar configuration. The pools are really too big, and at moderate levels of water availability there is no way to fill a few small pools more deeply while leaving other pools dry. Managers are left with no alternative but to expose large surfaces of water to the air. Hence it is not too surprising that evapotranspiration accounts for 95 percent of the water loss from the Bottoms, especially when you add the influences of wind and high summer temperatures. For a fixed volume of water, of course, doubling the depth of the pool would halve the rate of evaporation. Unfortunately the dikes were constructed with inadequate protection from the considerable wave action generated across the shallow, wind-swept surface of the pools. Therefore during periods of abundant water the pools cannot be filled to their design level of 4.5 feet, a depth that would accomplish a relative decrease in evaporative loss.

In times of overabundance of water, the flatness of the terrain within the basin ensures that water will flood peripheral private lands. The basin flooded before the development of the wildlife area, but recently, the Department of Wildlife and Parks has been held accountable by adjacent landowners (as you might expect in this adversarial age) because of the lack of deep storage and the inability to transfer water rapidly into the outlet canal.

Water loss between the Dundee diversion dam and the Bottoms can be as much as 80 percent. Given the present competition for groundwater and its impact on surface flow, the Arkansas River as a reliable source of water for the future is so improbable that solving problems associated with its use should have the lowest priority. If water in the Walnut Creek watershed were to become more

Aerial view of Cheyenne Bottoms, looking east with the inlet canal extending along the right.

The white-faced ibis captures a variety of invertebrates with its stout, decurved bill.

The predaceous raccoon is an important link in the detritivore-decomposer pathway.

Once almost extirpated from North America, the great egret has responded to protection.

Its feathers erect, a wintering western meadowlark insulates its body against further heat loss.

Abundant during migration, a few northern pintails linger at the Bottoms to breed.

The cryptic plumage of the American bittern matches the mottled patterns of the marsh.

Thousands of green-winged teal pass through in March, evading competition with later arriving shorebird flocks.

Although some of these American white pelicans sport nuptial knobs, none breed at the Bottoms.

American avocets in nuptial plumage.

A great blue heron scavenges fish stranded by the summer drawdown.

The russet "ear" patch and barred breast are diagnostic for the stilt sandpiper in spring.

The coyote is an opportunistic predator, invading aquatic communities during the summer retreat of water.

The ring-billed gull is a visitor to the Bottoms as long as open water remains.

Lesser yellowlegs are abundant in the marsh during their periods of passage.

available, however, the problem of water loss from the inlet channel would have to be solved.

THE TRAGEDY OF THE COMMONS

Given the context of the inadequacy of water in the history of cultural development on the High Plains, it should be no surprise that the lack of water is the major problem threatening the continued existence of Cheyenne Bottoms. The all too frequent picture of the Bottoms as a plain of drying mud, the cracked polygons strewn with the carcasses of carp shimmering with maggots in the summer sun, is the consequence of a perfectly natural situation. The average annual precipitation in Great Bend is 24.7 inches with about three-fourths of the rain falling between April and September. Although evapotranspiration from marsh vegetation is in balance with rainfall, water lost from native grasses in the surrounding prairies exceeds precipitation by 3 inches; about 60 inches is lost each year by evaporation from open water surfaces. This water deficit is lessened by the flows of Blood and Deception creeks into Cheyenne Bottoms, but this is a limited asset since their combined collecting basins total a mere 105 square miles. Accordingly, this surface flow is often less than 20 percent of the import from direct rainfall. Furthermore, in low precipitation years, no stream flow in the watershed reaches the wetland areas, and only in high precipitation years will this surface runoff actually reach the boundary of the wildlife area. It is estimated that through the ages the Bottoms has had water only two years out of every five.

At the other extreme, nine major floods have occurred from 1885 to 1980, sometimes causing the Bottoms to become a large lake covering at least 20,000 acres by the most conservative estimate. In 1928 the level became high enough so that water actually overflowed the basin and ran out Little Cheyenne Creek, a channel that had been little used since the end of the Pleistocene.

The hope to manage the water level at Cheyenne Bottoms began with L. Baldwin, superintendent of schools in Great Bend during the 1880s, who suggested that water could be diverted from the Arkansas River. George and Ed Moses and J. V. Brinkman became interested in this possibility and formed the Grand Lake Reservoir Company in 1897. The company hired F. B. Koen and George A. Trites, both of whom had been involved in diversion projects in eastern Colorado, to supervise the construction of a ditch from the river near Dundee to the Bottoms. Land for this canal was obtained by condemnation, and there was considerable agitation in response to the settlements proposed. Finally all the necessary land was acquired. In the interim, the company had been reorganized by W. J. Hallack of Kansas City as the Lake Koen Navigation, Reservoir, and Irrigation Company. In February 1899 water flowed from the Arkansas River to Cheyenne Bottoms for the first time. Mr. Koen was enthusiastically optimistic over this success and was quoted in the May 19, 1899, issue of the Barton County Democrat newspaper: "The lake will be a good deal more than simply a storage reservoir. Hotels and boat houses will be built on the banks and pleasure steamers will ply on the waters of this restored sea. I expect to put a steamer on there that will carry a thousand." Understatement is not the way of land promoters. Despite the flood of 1902 that washed out the diversion dam, this system, like all the other contemporary river diversion schemes, was doomed to failure because of too many ditches and too little surface flow; it was a brief act in the tragedy of the commons. In the meantime, in the words of one historian, "Mr. Koen blew back into eastern Colorado with a dusty Kansas wind." In fact, he went all the way to Arizona.

The desire to save the Bottoms is not a new cause. There was pressure early in this century to drain the Bottoms once and for all so that the area could be farmed. At about the same time a plan was suggested to transfer water from the Smoky Hill River via Cow Creek, a precursor of contemporary proposals for water transfer from the haves to the have-nots within the state. But in 1925 the Kansas Forestry, Fish and Game Commission was created and assumed the responsibility for the development of the Bottoms. During the wet weather cycle of 1927–1928, the U.S. Department of the Interior even recommended that the Bottoms become the first site in the developing network of National Wildlife Refuges. In a plea for this proposal J. Burt Doze, state fish and game warden, wrote in 1928 that "between Canada and the Gulf there is no place for wild waterfowl to get a drink without endangering its life." Frank Robl of Ellinwood, who pioneered the banding of waterfowl at the Bottoms, was active in the quest for funding. It also helped that Charles Curtis of Topeka was then vice-president under Herbert Hoover. Legislation providing a quarter of a million dollars for this project was passed in 1930, but when actual funding decreased to a fifth of this amount as a result of the need to initiate development of the Bear River refuge in Utah, the project was abandoned. It is ironic that Cheyenne Bottoms, an area currently faced with too little water, lost out to Bear River, a site recently obliterated by too much water as a result of the rising level of the Great Salt Lake.

With the passage of the Federal Aid to Wildlife Restoration [Pittman-Robertson] Act in 1937, money from taxes on firearms and ammunition made it possible to attempt the development of the Bottoms as a public wildlife area.

The diversion dam spans the dry, sandy bottom of the Arkansas River at Dundee, waiting for the spring flood.

Beginning in 1949, canals, dikes, control structures, roads, and blinds were built, and the area was opened to hunting in 1952. In 1957 the diversion dam on the Arkansas River was completed, and the system of canals and diversion dams on Walnut and Dry Walnut creeks directed water into the Bottoms, generally following the route developed by Koen at the end of the previous century. I doubt if any of the proponents for this new diversion scheme had forgotten the lessons of the past. Perhaps they hoped that since river diversion had proven fruitless in meeting the demands of agriculture, there would at least be sufficient flow to satisfy the needs of wildlife. Center pivot irrigation had yet to be implemented when this diversion plan was instigated. How could its supporters have foreseen the myopic lack of holistic heed in its use or appreciated its subversive impact on the environment? Nevertheless, this water supplementation system was completed just in time to be rendered ineffective by the increased dewatering of the Ogallala aquifer.

As irrigation depresses the water table in the form of an inverted cone around the base of each well, water flows away from nearby rivers toward these sinks; surface flow in the river bed goes down and then falls out of sight. The Arkansas River at Kinsley now carries less than 5 percent of the flow that it carried in the 1940s. Although fluctuating as a result of wet and dry periods during the 1960s, flow in Walnut Creek has also tended to drop since the mid-1970s. Since 1958, however, precipitation in most years has been above normal. Hence the decline in flow of both the Arkansas River and Walnut Creek is clearly the result of the lowering of water tables in their drainage basins by groundwater mining. Additionally, reduced runoff has resulted from conservation techniques to preserve water where it is needed for crop production, like terracing which began in the 1940s and the building of small watershed impoundments which peaked in the 1980s.

The small dams, however, do not appear to cause a significant reduction in the volume of water in Walnut Creek available for diversion, although 40 percent of its original flow is no longer obtainable because of conservation practices. The present management scheme for the Bottoms was conceptually valid but has failed in the face of increased competition for the water in the commons. Those practices which Marsha Marshall of the Kansas Water Authority has called the "commodification of nature" have left Cheyenne Bottoms with just the irregular and meager rainfall as its only significant source of water, and that source is insufficient in most years.

GLOBAL WARMING

As glacial ice is formed in alpine, arctic, and antarctic regions, small bubbles of air are trapped, encapsulating a
sample from the earth's atmosphere at the time of preservation. Analysis of this air in bubbles dating back to the
middle of the last century gives a concentration for carbon
dioxide of 0.028 percent. Even though 1850 was a hundred
years after the beginning of the industrial revolution, the
world was still largely agrarian. In 1958 direct observations of the carbon dioxide concentration in the atmosphere were initiated on the peak of Mauna Loa in Hawaii,
far from the highly populated regions of the world, but a
world far more industrialized than in 1850. At that time
carbon dioxide made up 0.032 percent of the atmosphere,
and by 1984 the level had climbed to 0.034 percent. At the
current exponential rates of increase, which in absolute
terms now equals 2.5 to 3 billion tons per year, the most
conservative estimates predict that the concentration of
carbon dioxide will double toward the end of the next century.

Even though these changes seem numerically minuscule, the effect of this change on the energy budget of the
planet is tremendous. Carbon dioxide is transparent to incoming solar radiation, but a portion of this energy is reflected from the surface of the earth toward deep space as
infrared radiation. Carbon dioxide absorbs infrared wavelengths and emits these long wavelengths back toward the
surface; hence that heat is not lost to outer space but is
retained within the lower atmosphere (the troposphere).
Ozone and other gases like methane and nitrous oxide,
which are naturally produced in marshes like Cheyenne
Bottoms as well as through our industrial culture, have
the same effect; so do the man-made chlorofluorocarbons
(which are also involved in another serious environmental

problem, the depletion of upper atmosphere ozone). Their concentrations are also increasing and will eventually have an impact equal to or greater than that of carbon dioxide. All these gases behave like the glass in a greenhouse, allowing penetration of solar energy but reflecting radiant heat; hence the term "greenhouse effect."

There is nothing speculative about the greenhouse effect; it was described by the French mathematician Fourier in the eighteenth century and quantified by Svante Arrhenius in the nineteenth century. Nor is the rise in atmospheric carbon dioxide conjecture; it is an empirical fact. What is controversial, however, is the projection for future change. According to some estimates, greenhouse gases may double as early as 2050. Considerable difference in opinion also exists regarding the consequences of this increase in the greenhouse gases on global climate. James E. Hansen of NASA's Goddard Institute of Space Studies is 99 percent confident that the current warming trend, which has produced the six warmest years of the last century during the 1980s, is the direct effect of the increase in greenhouse gases. Some climatologists, on the other hand, do not *yet* proclaim such a cause-and-effect relationship—but they all agree that it will come.

The exponential increase in carbon dioxide results without doubt from the burning of fossil fuels, which supply 80 percent of the world's energy demands. In recent years, accelerated burning of the tropical forests has also contributed carbon dioxide to the atmosphere. The other greenhouse gases are similarly anthropogenic in their origin and are increasing at even greater rates. What is not certain is how these rates of production will continue. The earth will get warmer. But how much warmer? Estimates vary from 2 to 6 degrees C for a doubling of the concentration of the greenhouse gases; the unknown variables include the role of the oceans as reservoirs for carbon diox-

117

ide and heat, the effect of cloud cover either as a reflector of incoming solar radiation or as a heat blanket, and possible changes in the amount and distribution of precipitation. Since vegetation converts atmospheric carbon dioxide into organic compounds through photosynthesis, future rates of global deforestation must also be considered because there is about as much carbon stored in the world's forests as there is in the atmosphere.

Even the maximum estimates for global warming are within the range of temperature change actually experienced since the middle of the last glacial advance. What is uniquely different, however, is the rate at which this change will occur: anywhere from ten to forty times faster than the warming that occurred during the postglacial hypsithermal. The sediment cores from Cheyenne Bottoms reveal that this habitat was affected by this past warming trend, but it occurred over thousands of years. What are the consequences of a warming trend of the same magnitude over a period of probably less than one hundred years?

The effect of global warming is expected to increase the amount of rainfall, but most of this increase will occur at tropical latitudes. It is projected that total rainfall probably will decrease in the Great Plains, and the Arkansas drainage is considered to be the fourth most vulnerable watershed after those in the Great Basin, California, and the Missouri River. Even though more rain will fall on a global scale, more water will be lost through increased evaporation so that soil moisture levels will decrease, causing an increase of about 30 percent in the irrigation demand for crop production in the western United States. Global warming will accentuate the present geographic unevenness of surface temperatures, inducing a greater change at higher latitudes than in the tropics. For each one-degree increase in temperature, the global vegetation patterns

Even though "in compliance," the effluents from the burning of fossil fuels contribute to an exponential increase in the greenhouse gases.

will shift 100 to 150 kilometers north. Tropical biomes will increase in coverage, while boreal forests and tundras will shrink.

The present breeding grounds for most of the shore-birds that pass through Cheyenne Bottoms will be drastically reduced, and in some cases probably eliminated, but other areas may become available as the Greenland ice cap retreats. As a result of a reduction in arctic and antarctic ice, ocean levels will rise as much as 1.5 meters, which in turn may produce more wetlands across the coastal plains unless heroic efforts are marshalled to dike the continents. Weedy plants can probably keep up with the rapid changes in the geography of temperature patterns, but tree species and herbaceous perennials are less mobile, having evolved in more stable communities where distant seed dispersal is not necessarily advantageous. These trees and perennials and their offspring will stand rooted in the soil as the temperature increases engulf them; once they reach their limit of tolerance, they will die. Since trees have a dominant effect on community microclimate, other species of plants and animals will be adversely affected also. Generally, global biotic diversity is expected to decrease.

The Scientific Committee on Problems of the Environment, International Council of Scientific Unions, has commented that "many important economic and social decisions are being made today on long-term projects . . . all based on the assumption that past climatic data, without modification, are a reliable guide to the future. This is no longer a good assumption since the increasing concentrations of greenhouse gases are expected to cause a significant warming of the global climate in the next century." The future of Cheyenne Bottoms is not immune to the infectious disruptions arising from this acute perturbation in the environment. Ignoring the reality of global warming will put to naught any short-sighted attempts to save the Bottoms.

EPILOGUE

Perhaps the present water crisis in the Bottoms should have been predicted years ago, given the history of water use in the High Plains and the consequences of the tragedy of the commons. Yet it is our nature to attempt to surmount problems intrinsic to our environment by whatever technology seems currently most appropriate. For most of the years that the Bottoms has existed as a managed marsh, rainfall has been above normal and the decline in the water table had not reached an alarming rate. The technology chosen was working. Indeed, we do win some, and the quality of life is improved. We also lose some, some like the Bottoms that we thought we had won.

Although the lack of continued maintenance of the water distribution system to counteract siltation has generated its own set of problems, the real problem of the Bottoms is not enough water. Or is it? Perhaps the problem actually is our wrongful consideration of natural resources as income instead of as capital. Perhaps it is also the stubbornness of humankind in refusing to recognize that natural process cannot be ignored or circumvented by technological fiat, especially in the Great American Desert. Perhaps our arrogance has so greatly affected the water economy of the High Plains and the Arkansas valley in particular that the damage is irreparable. Furthermore, our disregard for the entire biosphere is steadily modifying the atmosphere of the planet toward ends that we might intellectually understand but still perhaps cannot quite assimilate into our daily behavior. If there is a solu-

The prairie sun bakes the mudflats of the Bottoms. The once-expected water now has found better uses, says wise man.

tion that will save the Bottoms, it must, of necessity, have ramifications that affect the agribusiness and infrastructure of the Arkansas valley and the lifestyles of people far beyond the High Plains. That includes you and me, wherever we are. Is Cheyenne Bottoms worth it? Perhaps.

8   The Importance

The second of the four Pleistocene glaciers reached Kansas around 700,000 years ago. The glacier made it just over the border, putting the crush of its icy thumbprint on only the northeast corner of the state, an area bounded by the Big Blue River on the west and by the Kaw on the south. The rest of Kansas is unglaciated. It is an old topography. Water, tumbling down from the snowmelt of the Rockies or scouring streams with the downpours of the June monsoon, has eroded the watersheds in its relentless compulsion to reach the sea, wearing down the channels and obliterating any ponds and lakes that filled basins when the landscape was younger. As a result, few natural lakes occur in Kansas and those exist only for geologically short periods of time as oxbows cut off by the meanderings of the major rivers or as rain-blessed playas in impervious basins scattered across the prairie.

Wetlands were scarce in Kansas thousands of years ago; they are even scarcer today. Within historic times there once may have been as many as twelve large marshes and two thousand small playa lakes in the state, but now only three of these extensive marsh complexes remain—Jamestown, Quivira, and Cheyenne Bottoms—and the numbers of smaller wetlands have been reduced also. Some compensation for this loss has resulted from the development of man-made marshes, for example, at

Perry Lake and the Marais des Cygnes Wildlife Management Areas. Since conservationists began keeping score, however, the state has lost nearly 50 percent of the wetlands that existed in 1950. Kansas, of course, is not unique. The natural wetlands in the United States were estimated to have once totaled 127 million acres, but by 1950 about 35 percent of these had been drained through the modification of the landscape in our search for a place to settle and make our living. By the early 1980s it was estimated that we had reached the halfway mark as wetlands diminished at a rate of 300,000 acres per year. Such losses finally reach a point that results in a negative feedback on the very agriculture, commerce, and industry that we were hoping to stimulate by the eradication of wetlands. Water is not a trivial commodity. Society's increasing concern about water may indicate that we perhaps have reached that point.

Because it had so few wetlands, especially marshes, to begin with, Kansas is usually not mentioned when the doleful roll call of wetland losses in the various states is enumerated. Certainly the reduction of wetlands has been greater in other states, close to 95 percent in Iowa and Illinois. But when you have less to start with, even smaller percentage reductions are devastating in terms of the absolute amount of habitat. This absolute amount of habitat, that is, the total resource space, determines the limits for wildlife populations. The migratory waterbirds depend on absolute quantities of seeds, bloodworms, microcrustaceans, and fish to fuel their travels across the sky for hundreds and even thousands of miles twice a year. Thus their lives can be balanced between the best possible place to rear young and the best possible place to sustain life until it comes time to breed again. These same resources support coot and heron, who sojourn in the marsh during the

Waterfowling in the Bottoms, a tradition that binds generations together.

growing season, as well as muskrat and mink, who must remain to survive the rigors of winter.

Like other wetlands in Kansas, Cheyenne Bottoms is an aberration in the landscape, an interruption in the monotonous expanse of prairies and agrosystems. Like the pearl which arises from an interruption to the oyster's serenity, Cheyenne Bottoms also has economic value. Historically it has been an important waterfowl hunting area, and in the early years of this century market hunters exported thousands of ducks to eastern cities. After the flood of 1927, which attracted large numbers of waterfowl, refrigerated box cars were sent to Great Bend to return the huge harvest to Kansas City and beyond. Since the Bottoms came under state control, as many as 600,000 ducks and 40,000 geese have been on the area simultaneously during fall migration, an attractive resource for the sport hunter. Accordingly, when water levels are satisfactory, large numbers of hunters come to the Bottoms to obtain space in the blinds constructed in the perimeter pools on the north and east sides or to occupy shooting posts around the periphery.

The economic survey conducted over the hunting season in 1985 and 1986 as part of the environmental assessment showed that the teal season accounted for 1,911 person-days of use and duck and goose hunting totaled 3,833 person-days. These values translate into a total of $128,188 spent for travel and equipment by waterfowl hunters in just the local economy of Barton County. The pheasant population in the Bottoms also attracts hunters who spent an estimated 1,246 person-days at that sport and provided $33,715 to the local economy. Day use by birdwatchers, however, exceeds that of all bird hunters by a factor greater than two, equalling a total of 15,568 person-days. The primary impact of this nonconsumptive activity on the Barton County economy was estimated at $606,195, almost four times that of waterfowl and pheasant hunters combined.

When the primary input into the Kansas economy from recreational activities at the Bottoms is determined, along with the estimated secondary, ripple effects on goods and services, the combined total for all activities, including expenditures of the state to maintain this facility, equals $2,808,787 per year. Of this grand total, the state expends only about 8.3 percent in providing for the generation of the remainder of this $3 million—not a bad return on investment. Waterfowl hunting contributes 16.3 percent, and pheasant hunting, 3.7 percent. Birdwatching, on the other hand, accounts for 67.7 percent of the total. All other activities that could be measured—deer hunting, miscellaneous environmental study, and fishing—account for the remaining 4 percent. The attractiveness of Cheyenne Bottoms as an environmental resource to a great many people engaging in both consumptive and nonconsumptive uses has a significant economic impact,

"Look, third dowitcher from the left, doesn't it have spots on the flanks?" But Leann is still searching for the sora on the other side of the dike.

both locally and throughout the entire state. This revelation surprised a few people.

Similarly, it has been only quite recently that concerned people have come to realize the critical importance of Cheyenne Bottoms in the economy of nature. This wetland is now recognized as essential for the continued existence of many populations of migratory birds. Part of this latency, I suspect, comes from the bias of most people against the possibility that anything of importance could happen in Kansas! But as far as documenting the centrality of Cheyenne Bottoms to hemispheric bird populations, Kansans themselves are remiss. Historically, the state wildlife agency has not been able to devote much of its limited budget to basic research. Since its income once came solely from license fees, its obligation to concentrate on what was huntable and fishable (and to confine its focus within the political borders) is understandable. Some individuals certainly suspected that the Bottoms had at least regional and perhaps continental importance for the welfare of migrating waterbirds but had little opportunity within the strictures of their job descriptions to pursue those hypotheses. Nor have the academic ornithologists in the state done more than contribute to the checklist, substantiate records with specimens, and bring their classes to the Bottoms. The hemispheric-wide implications of Cheyenne Bottoms have come about largely from the avocational dedication of amateur ornithologists who were curious about the movements of birds using the Bottoms.

Frank W. Robl, who farmed at Ellinwood, began banding birds at Cheyenne Bottoms in 1924 and continued this hobby for over a quarter of a century. By 1939 he had banded 18,842 birds; a little over 85 percent were ducks, from which he obtained 2,500 band recoveries. In 1933, Frederick C. Lincoln of the Bureau of Biological Survey, the forerunner of the U.S. Fish and Wildlife Service, reported on Mr. Robl's records. His analysis illustrated that Cheyenne Bottoms was a central stopover point for ducks nesting as far to the northwest as Alaska and the Mackenzie valley and east to the prairie provinces and the northern plains states. Waterfowl passing through the Bottoms went west to California, east to the coast of South Carolina, and south to Louisiana and Texas, Cuba, Mexico, and even Honduras. Mr. Robl maintained a continued interest in wildlife and was an active voice for its conservation as long as he lived.

Probably one of the more important things I have done in my life was to write a letter to the Bird-banding Laboratory of the U.S. Fish and Wildlife Service in support of Edmund Martinez's request for a banding permit. Ed Martinez is an entomologist working for the Kansas State Extension Service, but like Frank Robl, he was curious about the migratory patterns of the birds at the Bottoms, especially the shorebirds. Prior to Ed's efforts only 349 shorebirds of 16 species had been banded in all of North America! From 1966 through 1978, he banded 58,159 individuals of 32 species by going out daily during migration and setting his nets two hours before sunrise, then taking them down about an hour after sunrise in order to begin his regular full-time job. Of the total banded, 50 percent were semipalmated sandpipers, many of which were subsequently recovered on their Alaskan breeding grounds as well as on their Brazilian wintering range. Northernmost recoveries are for a long-billed dowitcher and pectoral sandpiper from central Siberia; the southernmost is a white-rumped sandpiper from Argentina. Because of the large numbers of birds banded and the continuity of his data for over a decade of effort, Ed's work became of singular importance in the growing awareness by professional ornithologists and conservationists of the strategic importance of Cheyenne Bottoms as a focal stopover point in the hemispheric movement of shorebirds, which as a group have the longest migratory journeys of any bird.

In 1974 the International Shorebird Survey was organized, and Brian Harrington of the Manomet Bird Observatory in Massachusetts, along with his network that grew to over 500 volunteer cooperators, conducted a systematic survey of North American shorebird populations east of the 105th meridian, about the longitude of the Rocky Mountains. They also surveyed less intensely covered areas in the western states and Central and South America. The principal purposes of this effort were to identify traditional migratory stopover sites, document their use, illustrate their importance, and predict the vulnerability of shorebirds to the loss of these areas. Ed Martinez donated his time and effort to do the counts at Cheyenne Bottoms during the fall from 1976 to 1983 and in the spring from 1980 to 1983. As with all the other volunteers, this was no minor task since it involved conducting numerical counts by species every ten days over a total of four months of each year.

The results of this survey coupled with other reports revealed that the number of major stopover places throughout the whole Western Hemisphere is very small, just three sites east of the Rockies, just five sites west of the Rockies, and just five sites in Central and South America. There may be other undiscovered areas, but the corollary of this finding is shocking. The continued existence of shorebird populations, which number in the millions, may depend on a mere handful of geographic foci without which these birds will be unable to make the migratory journeys upon which their life cycles pivot. Furthermore, most of these critical staging areas are located precariously close to potential disruption by humans, either from direct competition for resources or from the impacts of pollution. The mudflats on the Bay of Fundy could be sacrificed to generate electrical power for the eastern grid by harnessing the famous tidal bore. Cheyenne Bottoms may become permanently dry, its source of water entirely preempted by the need to maintain the forage-to-beef-to-packing-plant-to-fastfood-hamburger commercial pathway. The proper salinity of the marine estuary of San Francisco Bay is continually threatened by diversion of freshwater inflow, and the habitat suffers modification through diking and filling. The timing of shorebird migration along the Atlantic coast has evolved so that the birds' arrival at Delaware Bay is coincident with the peak of egg-laying by horseshoe crabs. But ocean transport of production and product, feeding the petrochemical complex of Philadelphia and Wilmington, passes within sight of these sandy shores. One major spill at the wrong time could be catastrophic. The Copper River Delta lies immediately south of Valdez, Alaska; recent history documents the dangers along that tanker sealane.

The banding records of Ed Martinez at Cheyenne Bottoms, Peter Hicklin in the Bay of Fundy, and others elsewhere have demonstrated that these staging areas are traditional; individual birds return year after year to the same place during the course of their migratory passage. The stereotypy of their behavior offers minimal adaptability in the complex neural network that directs their still mysterious navigational systems. Obviously if the habitat is unsuitable, the birds go elsewhere, as they must do, for example, when the Bottoms is dry. We do find shorebirds invading ephemeral habitats like flooded fields when suitable sites are abundant, so their behavior is not utterly rigid. But what do they do when suitable sites are scarce? Do they fly over the traditional staging area until exhaustion forces them down in submarginal habitat? We don't know, but it is a reasonable hypothesis that these alternate sites are probably nowhere near as rich in food resources or as protected from predation as the traditional areas. J. P. Myers argues that areas like Cheyenne Bottoms are the traditional staging sites because they were the only optimally acceptable sites in the region, even before the anthropogenic reduction in the availability of wetlands. Clearly, the continued existence of these few vulnerable links in the chain of wetlands that sustain migratory shorebirds is critical.

Cheyenne Bottoms stands alone in the center of the continent as the most significant staging area for the migration of shorebirds. During the Manomet survey no other site censused in the Great Plains from Texas to North Dakota had even 10 percent of the number of shorebirds that were counted at Cheyenne Bottoms. During the spring, of the 210 sites surveyed east of the 105th meridian, an average of 45 percent of the total shorebirds counted were at Cheyenne Bottoms. In the fall, of the 454 sites across the same region, 28 percent of the shorebirds were counted at Cheyenne Bottoms. At the species level the importance of Cheyenne Bottoms is even more striking. During the spring passage, over 90 percent of the total individuals counted east of the 105th meridian for white-rumped, Baird's, and stilt sandpipers, long-billed dowitcher, and Wilson's phalarope were at the Bottoms. Since the major migratory routes of the latter two species lie west of the survey region, the percentages of the continental population for dowitchers and phalaropes passing through the Bottoms are probably lower. Yet the numbers are still substantial.

Spring numbers also indicated that 74 percent of the pectoral sandpipers, 73 percent of the marbled godwits, and 59 percent of the Hudsonian godwits passed through the area. In the fall, the numbers of long-billed dowitchers were again above the 90 percent mark. The fall statistics do not indicate that the Bottoms is less important for the flight south. Rather, these numbers reflect the broader pathways chosen by inexperienced birds, so the numbers are spread more widely across the continent. Single daily census records of 101,500 white-rumps, 62,580 Baird's, 210,000 long-billed dowitchers, and 130,000 Wilson's phalarope stand as emphatic testimonials to the importance of the Bottoms. Of the 31 species evaluated in the International Shorebird Survey, 20 species were present in numbers at Cheyenne Bottoms that exceeded 5 percent of the total count for all ISS sites. Indeed Brian Harrington suggests that Cheyenne Bottoms may be the most important stopover area for northern shorebirds in North America and perhaps the entire western hemisphere!

As a result of the International Shorebird Survey conducted by the Manomet Bird Observatory, a Western

Ring-billed gulls

Hemisphere Shorebird Reserve Network has been developed to emphasize the preservation of these critical wetlands. Cheyenne Bottoms is one of eleven locations in the Western Hemisphere currently included. In 1971 environmental leaders from around the world held a conference in Ramsar, Iran, concerning the conservation of global wetlands. As a result of these deliberations, a Convention on the Conservation of Wetlands of International Importance was developed and signed by 18 countries. The United States officially became party to this Convention on April 18, 1987, and in June 1988 the Kansas Department of Wildlife and Parks nominated Cheyenne Bottoms for inclusion under this convention as a Wetland of International Importance.

Kansas is one of the world's best kept secrets, and most of us like it that way. One of the negative aspects of this conspiracy, however, is that most Kansans often do not know the full extent of their blessings. The national and international recognition that has befallen Cheyenne Bottoms will not result in a deluge of extramural funds and a miraculous cure for its problems. What this notability does mean is that it is not just the local waterfowl hunters, birdwatchers, and tree-huggers who think Cheyenne Bottoms is worth saving; the whole world believes it.

9   Reprieve and Hope

REFORMATION AND RESTORATION

In her foreword to this book, Jan Garton recognized the ordinary people of Kansas who rose up and brought their concerns for Cheyenne Bottoms to the statehouse door, demanded a reformation in the priorities of the state wildlife agency, and made the development of a plan for the restoration of the Bottoms a possibility. Saving the Bottoms is still a hope, and the governor, the legislature, and the Department of Wildlife and Parks have made the commitment to stand with these people and develop a management strategy to increase the probability that Cheyenne Bottoms will continue to exist.

A twenty-five year plan is currently under development, and a pattern is already emerging. It is recognized that major supplementation from the Arkansas River is not possible; although in times of flood, water for diversion to the inlet canal will be available. Although surface water rights for diversion from the Arkansas to Cheyenne Bottoms were obtained in 1954, the legal labyrinth is a tangled knot that even bold Alexander could not cut. There is scant flow in Walnut Creek except during flood events, but the potential for increasing this source of water in the near future is very real since Cheyenne Bottoms has senior water rights and the number of competing appropriations is relatively small. Under pressure from the public (especially the Kansas Wildlife Federation), the

Department of Wildlife and Parks will pursue legal means to obtain whatever is available of the 20,000 acre-feet per year that was appropriated for diversion from Walnut Creek on October 8, 1948. If this litigation is successful, irrigation in the Walnut valley will be reduced by holders of junior water rights, and hydrological models predict a resultant increase in surface flow. These farmers will be negatively affected, perhaps even forced out of business; hence such action should not be considered lightly. But wildlife would benefit. Concurrent effort will be made to increase the integrity of the inlet channel so that loss through seepage and evaporation can be substantially reduced. Thus there is hope to restore some degree of water supplementation for the Bottoms. This will not come easily, nor will it be concluded rapidly.

More immediately, a protocol to enhance the use of the water from precipitation, both direct and through the watersheds of Blood and Deception creeks as well as from occasional diversion, is being considered, predicated on a thorough hydrological study of the basin. More adequate earth-moving and dredging equipment to keep barrow ditches and water control structures free of sediment has already been acquired, partly from funds donated by individual Kansans. Dependence on gravity flow for water distribution among the pools may be replaced by incorporating more pumping stations into the water distribution system. Some of the present pools could be subdivided so that greater selectivity in water delivery as well as draining could be realized. This possibility would facilitate cattail control, water conservation, and the seeding of annual grains for waterfowl. The feasibility of increasing the volume of the individual pools to enhance storage while decreasing relative evaporation will depend on the results of the hydrological study. The higher hydrostatic pressure resulting from such a modification could increase the volume of seepage, resulting in even greater net losses of water. Separate reservoirs dedicated to water storage may be necessary.

The management plan will of necessity consider the regions of the basin peripheral to the state-owned wildlife area and incorporate them into the overall strategy, either by direct purchase or the obtaining of easements. This will not only permit enhanced water storage and augment the availability of wetland habitats but will also eliminate the threat of litigation that has affected past water distribution procedures. The Department of Wildlife and Parks hopes to restore some of the wetlands in the Arkansas lowlands even though such a plan is not directly related to the management of the Bottoms. Thus alternate staging areas, especially for migrant shorebird populations, will be available when periodic drought decreases the suitability of the habitat in the basin of Cheyenne Bottoms.

The management plan for the Bottoms will also encompass visitor services so that access to the marsh will be facilitated, both for wildlife viewing as well as for waterfowl hunting. Additionally, an interpretive program will be implemented with the erection of a visitors' center and appropriate informational signs along dike roads and trails.

Probably the greatest reformation is the change in overall management strategy. For most of its existence, the Bottoms has been managed for waterfowl. That made considerable sense, since Pittman-Robertson funds and license fees created the wildlife area and supported its annual expenditures, but times have changed. Outdoor recreation involving wildlife has broadened beyond hook and bullet, and the greater citizen participation in nonconsumptive uses of wildlife compared to consumptive uses and their greater economic effects have been recognized. The Department of Wildlife and Parks, like the agencies in other states across the nation, now recognizes the importance of nongame wildlife programs in their overall mission. Furthermore, avenues for economic support by nonconsumptive users have become available through general revenue funds and especially through direct donations to nongame wildlife by means of the "chickadee check-off" or similar mechanisms on state income tax returns.

The management plan proposed for the Bottoms will be concerned for the welfare of all wildlife. Water distribution procedures will selectively control the levels of the various pools to permit optimal development of habitat for shorebirds during the seasons of their passage, for migrant and wintering waterfowl, and for nesting marsh birds like rails, herons, and ducks. Procedures for improving the suitability of the habitat for critical species will also be implemented, for example, constructing shallow nesting mounds for breeding least terns. Habitats will be manipulated to maintain a level of diversity that will sustain plant and animal populations characteristic of the various ecological communities in the basin. In short, Cheyenne Bottoms could become a significant biotic reserve as a result of a panoply of purposeful efforts rather than by the chance spin-off from single-purpose waterfowl management. Whether these improvements can be carried out and maintained for the long term, however, depends on a much broader environmental perspective.

THE ADVENT OF THE ENVIRONMENTAL REVOLUTION

Tom Lovejoy, formerly with the World Wildlife Fund and now secretary for external affairs of the Smithsonian Institution, has written, "I am utterly convinced that most of the great environmental struggles will be either won or lost in the 1990's, and that by the next century it will be too late to act." The gravity of Lovejoy's pronouncement

Least terns

takes awhile to penetrate the depths of our minds, since denial of doom is our protection against anxiety and our historical context tends to work along linear time scales and not with exponential rates of change. But the immediacy of his statement should not escape those of you who have come with me this far in the story of Cheyenne Bottoms. Indeed, for the Bottoms, the time is now. It is reasonable to suppose that the Bottoms is the notable bellwether of environmental degradation at least in the Great American Desert, if not for the entire continent. Saving Cheyenne Bottoms cannot be limited to the horizons of its basin. Maintaining this wetland demands substantial, sacrificial changes in the warp and woof of the very fabric of our life-styles, wherever we might live. Lest you consider

141

this overheated rhetoric, William Ruckelshaus has cautioned us that the revolution necessary to obtain adequate repair and protection in response to the misuses of the environment and to develop a sustainable ecological relationship between ourselves and the biosphere is comparable in its magnitude and ramifications to the Neolithic agricultural revolution or to the industrial revolution of the eighteenth century.

The center pivots will eventually bankrupt the capital investment accumulated over millions of years in the sands and gravels of the Ogallala since there is no volume of withdrawal that is sustainable in the face of an average recharge rate of half an inch or less per year. The whole agribusiness complex of the Kansas High Plains will be disrupted with a return to dryland cropping. Grass-fed beef production will become more prevalent, but bioenergetics dictates that cattle densities will of necessity be considerably less than could be maintained in high intensity feeding operations. Thus some, perhaps the majority, of the feedlots and meat processing plants will close along with the satellite businesses and service industries that have been necessary for their support, people will be deprived of their livelihoods, and western Kansas will see hard times reminiscent of the 1890s and the 1930s.

In 1976 Congress authorized the Six-state High Plains–Ogallala Aquifer Regional Resources Study as a result of growing concern about groundwater depletion. When the study was completed in 1982, Kansas was projected to suffer a reduction in its irrigated acreage from a high of 2.18 million in 1977 to 580,000 by 2020; that is a decrease of over 70 percent! In 1986 David Kromm and Stephen White reported, however, that only 30 percent of the residents in the High Plains thought that the economy would get worse. The subset of this survey that was composed of respondents from Texas, where groundwater failure is now more frequent, revealed greater pessimism, with 45 percent believing that their economy would decline, a reaction not paralleled in the other states. Experience is a good teacher.

Learning by trial and error is a common mechanism for nonhuman animals, even those as simple as single-celled protozoans. Humans, however, have the unique potential to predict their future on the basis of understanding and insight rather than on past experience, and thus can change the trajectory of their behavior. But as Tom Lovejoy has commented, "absence of widespread understanding of fundamental concepts about how the world works is at the heart of the general public, and hence of government, inability to address basic issues." One of a dozen recommendations arising from the High Plains–Ogallala study was that "further study should be given to local water supply augmentation." Kromm and White discovered that of all the recommendations, this was the one with which people living in the High Plains most agreed. One wonders from what local sources this augmentation would arise, and the response of these people suggests a level of naivete, if not ignorance, that validates Lovejoy's contention. Further substantiation of Lovejoy's observation is provided by the state government of Kansas, where there has been no action instigated by the legislature to prepare for this impending economic disaster, although some thought has been directed toward the problem under the umbrella of the state water plan. A century ago the wagons could return east and once hopeful settlers could regain economic stability after their defeat by the Great American Desert. In the 1930s, the Far West absorbed the desiccated dreams withered by the dust bowl. Where can we go this time?

Cassandra was not a pessimist; she was a realist, but the gods condemned her to the fate of not being believed.

Tom Lovejoy is also a realist, but we cannot afford a cred-
ibility gap, since more is at stake than one city on a hill.
Denial is the bandage we initially apply to cover real hurts,
but in time we accept the trauma and grow to a higher
level of maturity. The time for denial is past; we know that
even presidential edicts, like acid rain being good for
plants, are absurd. We must realistically face the situation
at hand so that the predictions of misfortune can define
the problems. Only then can we optimistically seek their
solutions. William C. Clark has recently written, "The
same wellsprings of human inventiveness and energy that
are so transforming the earth have also given us an un-
precedented understanding of how the planet works, how
our present activities threaten its workings, and how we
can intervene to improve the prospects for its sustainable
development." I hope so. Do we really have any other vi-
able alternative?

The suggested improvements for Cheyenne Bottoms
realistically recognize that restoration of flow in the Arkansas River will never reach a level that could reliably
supplement the water supply for the Bottoms during
droughts and that water in Walnut Creek will become
available only through extended legal strife. Even with a
return to dryland farming (as groundwater mining becomes no longer economically acceptable for crop production), the limited water supply for the High Plains will still
be under an array of competitive demands as we develop
other avenues for commerce and industry to replace those
lost to our present extravagance. The source of water for
the Bottoms is the sky above, not the ground below. Nor
is it Colorado. The USDA Soil Conservation Service currently concludes that at present sufficient water is available to maintain the Bottoms under average conditions. If
Cheyenne Bottoms is designed to gather as much water as

possible from rainfall, store as much water as possible from rainfall, conserve from evaporative loss as much of this water as possible, and manage water for the optimum benefit of wetland plants and animals during critical periods in their annual cycles, the contemporary water problems of the Bottoms will be lessened. We must expect, however, that during years when rainfall is below average (and there must always be many "below average" years to get an average), much of the Bottoms will be as dry as it was in the drought of 1988–1989. With the planned restoration of other historical wetlands in central Kansas, the availability of alternate staging areas may ease the impact of periodic droughts on migrant waterbirds.

These plans for the frugal use of water will also prepare us for the decrease in precipitation that will most assuredly come with global warming, although the timing and the intensity of the changes in both temperature and rainfall cannot be predicted with precision. These changes will come, of that we are sure; and if we do nothing to reduce their magnitudes, they will greatly curtail our ability to manage Cheyenne Bottoms. Therefore, we must immediately begin a concerted attack on the long-term causes of global warming if we are serious about the importance of maintaining Cheyenne Bottoms and other natural systems that support the biotic diversity of the planet. Solving some of the immediate problems at the Bottoms is easy; all it takes is money. Solving the long-term problem is more difficult. It will require a megametamorphosis in our life-style, in itself difficult enough, but this change also must be in response to future dangers that carry ill-defined probabilities rather than just to extant suffering. Governor Hayden of Kansas announced on October 28, 1989, that the Kansas Academy of Science will convene a governor's conference during the summer of 1990 to explore the possible adaptive responses to global climate change as it relates to Kansas. It is indeed time to mount the barricades and commence the revolution.

To lessen the consequences of global warming we have to reduce the exponential rate of increase in the greenhouse gases. That is, we must reduce our production of carbon dioxide, nitrous oxides, methane, and chlorofluorocarbons. It is important to recognize that many of the changes we must initiate to reduce these effluents of our culture will also ameliorate the other two critical and detrimental global changes going on in the biosphere—acid deposition and the widening of the hole in the ozone layer of the upper atmosphere. We must finally face the reality that burning fossil fuels, which produces carbon dioxide, nitrous oxides, and sulfur oxides, is dangerous. It is dangerous not for economic or geopolitical reasons; it is dangerous because it impinges on the ability of the biosphere to maintain its life-support functions. The immediate response to this danger means replacing coal, natural gas, and oil burners with nuclear power steam generators to produce electrical power and accepting risk levels for radionuclide waste storage with which we can literally live. In the longer term, we must develop a technology to harness the star on which the fire of life has always depended. Fission and fusion reactions produce environmental problems in both fuel production and in the disposal of radioactive wastes. Having the power-producing reactor 93 million miles away eliminates many detrimental environmental impacts. Solar power is our only long-term solution.

Decreasing the greenhouse gases also means reducing reliance on automobiles that use fossil fuels. The average American car driven the average American distance of 10,000 miles each year releases its own weight in carbon into the atmosphere as carbon monoxide and carbon dioxide. Considering the densities of automobiles on the Ventura or the Dan Ryan, or even Bluemont Avenue in Manhattan, Kansas, the amounts are not trivial. In the short term, car pooling must be the norm, and the reestablishment of mass transit for both urban and interurban transport must be enhanced. In fact, "highway funds" should be used to decrease highway use, not facilitate it. Reducing greenhouse gases means fewer 18-wheelers on the roads and a compensating return to the railroad. It means even better energy conservation than we attained under coercion by the OPEC cartel. For example, more energy still passes through the windows of buildings in the United States each year than flows south through the Alaska pipeline to Valdez. A decrease means ubiquitous recycling of mineral resources, of paper and wood products. It means less packaging for everything we use.

One of the secondary effects of tropical deforestation and the increase of dead wood is an increased abundance of termites. The guts of termites have a microbial flora that allows them to digest wood, but these creatures eliminate methane as a byproduct. Reducing the rate of deforestation thus can have a two-pronged effect on the decrease in the concentration of greenhouses gases; it would not only augment the removal of carbon dioxide from the atmosphere by photosynthetic fixation but also reduce termite-generated methane. The same microbial process occurs in the stomachs of ruminant livestock, which on a global scale produce 73 million metric tons of methane per year. But there's a catch-22 in any suggestion that beef production be substantially reduced since a compensatory increase in graminivory also affects the production of methane. The domesticated marshes of the world in which we cultivate rice, the grain many of the Earth's people rely on, produce 115 million tons of methane per year.

Solutions are not all "do nots"; there are some "dos."

For example, plant a tree. Two million square kilometers of forest will fix approximately one billion tons of carbon dioxide each year; that will lessen the current annual increase of carbon dioxide by over a third. Governor Hayden has directed the extension forestry department at Kansas State to implement a program for planting 2.4 million trees each year over the next ten years, specifically to reduce the rate of increase in atmospheric carbon dioxide. The federal government proposes to plant one billion trees a year. Similar strategies must become policy for all nations of the global community.

Substantial reduction of the atmospheric concentration of the greenhouse gases means disruption in jobs for thousands of good people who happen to be employed in industrial processes that will no longer be tenable. It means increased costs in doing business, hence increases in consumer prices. It means finally personally accepting the costs that for generations we have externalized by environmental degradation. It means learning to accept certain inconveniences that we once took for granted but have almost forgotten. It means shifting priorities for governmental expenditures so that local, national, and international environmental problems can be addressed. The recognition that the environmental revolution is now finally at hand comes at a most propitious moment. Admiral La Rocque, director of the Center for Defense Information, emphasized in a Lou Douglas lecture at Kansas State on October 3, 1989, that national security is far more dependent on a functional environment where citizens can live in good health and lead economically productive lives rather than on a system of filling missile silos with rockets we cannot use and building bombers we cannot see. The Cold War is over, but we are faced with battles to save the Earth that will be no less costly.

In the United States we profess environmental values,

but we practice the world's most wasteful and most polluting life-style. We and the rest of the wealthiest 15 percent of the world's population consume more than a third of the fertilizers and over half of the energy produced and hence are responsible for a major share of the deterioration in the global environment. Bill McKibben speaks of "the end of nature." Through this hyperbole he alerts us to how much of our total environment is man-created and therefore must be manipulated to sustain our lives. The natural environment has disappeared from much of our experience, attenuating our sensitivity to its degradation. Spaceship Earth has been crafted into an artificial world programmed for our survival, a space station. "We have built a greenhouse—a human creation—where once there bloomed a sweet and wild garden."

A quarter of the world's population goes to bed hungry during at least some seasons of the year. Thus economic development cannot be dismissed; technologies cannot be eliminated simply in order to reduce the environmental insults to our planet. As Prime Minister Brundtland of Norway has emphasized, global economic and global environmental concerns must be addressed together. An acceptable level of economic growth must be sustained so that prosperity and security can spread to disadvantaged sectors within countries as well as to less-developed nations, but the health of the biosphere must be maintained. Technologies must be resource-conserving, pollution-reducing, and perhaps even environment-restoring if we are to approach the next century with any degree of hope and confidence for future well-being. The costs for these endeavors will be borne largely by the developed nations, which probably demands that the wealthy minority will become less wealthy. But unlike Jack Benny, we cannot afford a long pause when given the choice between our money or our lives.

S. K. Majumder argues that the only way to restore the earth and make peace with nature is through a program of action that would convert our short-term preference for expediency into a long-term strategy for survival. Jacob Bronowski identifies the ethical context of such a shift in noting that "nothing erodes the public morality so much as the acquiescence in what is expedient when what is true is unpalatable." Myrl Duncan of the Washburn University Law School has emphasized the need for an "intergenerational justice" in our stewardship of the environment. Thankfully, the notion of a "just war" apparently has been extirpated from western thought in my lifetime. Although the environmental revolution will build rather than destroy, enhance life rather than eliminate life, the analogy to a "just war" seems appropriate. But a war to save our environment will be a relentless war and a difficult war.

The root cause of the environmental crisis is, of course, the exponential increase in the world's population. The current depletion of supplemental water for Cheyenne Bottoms resulting from the drawdown of the Ogallala and the impending water loss from reduced precipitation are effects arising directly from our demands on the biosphere to provide for increasing numbers of people. In 1850 there were only 1.25 billion people on the Earth. It took a hundred years for that number to double; the year I left home to enter Michigan State as a freshman there were only 2.5 billion people. Since that time the world's population has doubled again and will reach 8.5 billion by 2025. Most of these people will be living in the developing nations of the world, countries that have a critical need for continuing economic development. On September 14, 1989, Dr. Joseph Chamie, chief of the Population Policy Section of the United Nations Secretariat, spoke at Kansas State University on the global implications of these population

Northern pintails

changes and offered that the question to be addressed is "how to satisfy the increasing aspirations of the earth's growing population of more than 5 billion people, reduce the widening social and economic disparities both within and among countries, and at the same time safeguard the earth's natural resources, atmosphere and other critical components of the environment." How, indeed! That evening I had a chance to talk with Dr. Chamie, and I wanted the answer to only one question: Was he optimistic? He said yes.

In saving Cheyenne Bottoms we are faced with grave adversities that require a behavioral set for which we are poorly prepared genetically. It is not only survival of self and kin at risk; it is also the survival of the pleasing diversity of the planet on which all life depends. We must restore nature to some degree of independence, free of the fetters of humankind's debilitating manipulations. Saving Cheyenne Bottoms seems like such a small step, but I can think of no more appropriate place to focus our concerns. Cheyenne Bottoms has local, intrinsic value as a remnant wetland, and its importance to migratory wildlife has hemispheric implications. The changes in our behavior that would increase the chance for the continued existence of the Bottoms have ramifications that could improve the probabilities that other habitats, including those we depend on for food and fiber, will survive as well. Saving Cheyenne Bottoms is one small step in the environmental revolution, a revolution demanding that we divest ourselves of our innate egocentricity and make the leap of faith to behave in ways that benefit the entirety of life. At no time in the course of evolution has a true altruism been demanded in the struggle for existence. Saving Cheyenne Bottoms is one small step, but can we take it? Can we at last embark on a humane evolutionary journey? I am convinced that we can.

Bibliography

1 "AN INSUPERABLE OBSTACLE"

Bittinger, M. W., and E. B. Green. 1980. You Never Miss the Water Till . . . (The Ogallala Story). Water Resources Publications, Littleton, CO.

Coues, E. 1895. The Expeditions of Zebulon Montgomery Pike (vol. 2). Francis P. Harper, New York.

Duncan, M. 1986. New ethic needed to sustain High Plains agriculture. Kansas Nat. Res. Council Jour. 5(3): 1, 4.

Foth, V. 1988. Water and the Making of Kansas. Kansas Natural Resource Council, Topeka.

Green, D. E. 1973. Land of the Underground Rain. Univ. Texas Press, Austin.

Hardin, G. 1968. The tragedy of the commons. Science 162: 1243–48.

Hollon, W. E. 1966. The Great American Desert. Then and Now. Oxford Univ. Press, New York.

Janovy, J., Jr. 1980. Yellowlegs. St. Martin's Press, New York.

Kromm, D. E., and S. E. White. 1981. Public perception of groundwater depletion in southwestern Kansas. Project Completion Report. Kansas Water Resources Research Instit., Manhattan.

———. 1986. Variability in adjustment preferences to groundwater depletion in the American High Plains. Water Resources Bull. 22: 791–801.

———. 1987. Interstate groundwater management preference differences: The Ogallala region. Jour. Geography, Jan.–Feb.: 5–11.

Madson, C. 1981. Goodbye to the Ark. Kansas Wildlife 38 (4): 24–31.

Mathews, B. 1980. Water crisis on the plains. Kans. Fish and Game 37 (3): 27–31.

Miner, C. 1986. West of Wichita. Settling the High Plains of Kansas, 1865–1890. Univ. Press of Kansas, Lawrence.

Smith, H. N. 1950. Virgin Land. The American West as Symbol and Myth. Harvard Univ. Press, Cambridge, MA.

Taylor, J. E. 1964. Water, our prime natural resource. Kans. Hist. Quart. 30: 112–19.

Thwaites, R. G. 1905. Early Western Travels 1748–1846. Vol. 16, part III and Vol. 17, part IV of James's Account of S. H. Long's Expedition, 1819–1820. A. H. Clark, Cleveland.

Tomayko, J. E. 1983. The ditch irrigation boom in southwest Kansas: Changing an environment. Jour. of the West 22 (2): 20–25.

Udall, S. 1987. To the Inland Empire. Coronado and Our Spanish Legacy. Doubleday, New York.

Webb, W. P. 1931. The Great Plains. Ginn and Company, Boston.

2 THE BASIN

Bardack, D. 1962. A review of the fossil birds of Kansas. Kans. Ornithol. Soc. Bull. 13: 9–14.

Bare, J. E., and R. L. McGregor. 1970. An introduction to the phytogeography of Kansas. Univ. Kansas Sci. Bull. 48: 869–949.

Bayne, C. K. 1977. Geology and structure of Cheyenne Bottoms, Barton County, Kansas. Kans. Geol. Surv. Bull. 211 (part 2): 1–12.

Bennett, D. K. 1984. Fossils. In Kansas Geology, ed. R. Buchanan, pp. 96–162. Univ. Press of Kansas, Lawrence.

Coues, E. 1895. The Expeditions of Zebulon Montgomery Pike (vol. 2). Francis P. Harper, New York.

Gilfillan, M. 1988. Magpie Rising. Pruett Publ. Co., Boulder, CO.

Griffith, M., and G. Welker. 1987. Introduction. In Cheyenne Bottoms. An Environmental Assessment. Kans. Biol. Survey and Kans. Geol. Survey, Lawrence, pp. 1–13.

Latta, B. F. 1950. Geology and ground-water resources of Barton and Stafford counties, Kansas. Kansas Geol. Surv. Bull. 88: 1–228.

Miller, M. 1988. The way it was. Kansas Wildlife & Parks 45(4): 32–35.

Sadeghipour, J., and T. McClain. 1987. Analysis of surface-water and climatic data for Cheyenne Bottoms. In Cheyenne Bottoms. An Environmental Assessment. Kans. Biol. Survey and Kans. Geol. Survey, Lawrence, pp. 55–90.

Sophocleous, M., and R. Shapiro. 1987. Water balance of Cheyenne Bottoms, Kansas. In Cheyenne Bottoms. An Environmental Assessment. Kans. Biol. Survey and Kans. Geol. Survey, Lawrence, pp. 93–120.

Volger, L., G. Fredlund, and W. Johnson. 1987. Cheyenne Bottoms geology. In Cheyenne Bottoms. An Environmental Assessment. Kans. Biol. Survey and Kans. Geol. Survey, Lawrence, pp. 15–29.

Vogler, L., and T. McClain. 1987. Ground water hydrology. In Cheyenne Bottoms. An Environmental Assessment. Kans. Biol. Survey and Kans. Geol. Survey, Lawrence, p. 91.

Wells, P. V. 1970. Postglacial vegetational history of the Great Plains. Science 167: 1574–82.

3 WATER

Castro, G., F. L. Knopf, and B. A. Wunder. 1990. The drying of a wetland. Amer. Birds, in press.

Sadeghipour, J., and T. McClain. 1987. Analysis of surface-water and climatic data for Cheyenne Bottoms. In Cheyenne Bottoms. An Environmental Assessment. Kans. Biol. Survey and Kans. Geol. Survey, Lawrence, pp. 55–90.

Sophocleous, M., and R. Shapiro. 1987. Water balance of Cheyenne Bottoms, Kansas. In Cheyenne Bottoms. An Environmental Assessment. Kans. Biol. Survey and Kans. Geol. Survey, Lawrence, pp. 93–120.

Van der Valk, A. G. 1981. Succession in wetlands: A Gleasonian approach. Ecology 62: 688–96.

Vogler, L., M. Sophocleous, and T. McClain. 1987. Streamflow diversions and inlet canal performance. In Cheyenne Bottoms. An Environmental Assessment. Kans. Biol. Survey and Kans. Geol. Survey, Lawrence, pp. 49–162.

Weller, M. W., and L. H. Fredrickson. 1973. Avian ecology of a managed glacial marsh. Living Bird 12: 269–91.

Whittemore, D. O., and D. G. Huggins. 1987. Water quality. In Cheyenne Bottoms. An Environmental Assessment. Kans. Biol. Survey and Kans. Geol. Survey, Lawrence, pp. 31–54.

4 THE MARSH

Barry, L. 1972. The Beginning of the West. Kansas State Hist. Soc., Topeka.

Besser, J. F., and D. K. Steffen. 1988. Breeding and wintering areas of red-winged blackbirds banded in Barton County, Kansas. Kansas Ornithol. Soc. Bull. 39: 33–36.

Bradbury, I. K., and J. Grace. 1983. Primary production in wetlands. In Ecosystems of the World, 4A, Mires: swamp, bog, fen and moor, ed. A. J. P. Gore, pp. 285–310. Elsevier Sci. Publ. Co., Amsterdam, NETH.

Bray, J. R. 1962. Estimates of energy budget for a *Typha* (cattail) marsh. Science 136: 1119–20.

Brooks, R. E., and C. Kuhn. 1987. The vegetation of Cheyenne Bottoms. In Cheyenne Bottoms. An Environmental Assessment. Kans. Biol. Survey and Kans. Geol. Survey, Lawrence, pp. 251–315.

Cooper, E. L. 1987. Carp in North America. Amer. Fisheries Soc., Bethesda, MD.

Crawford, R. M. M. 1983. Root survival in flooded soils. In Ecosystems of the World, 4A, Mires: swamp, bog, fen and moor, ed. A. J. P. Gore, pp. 257–83. Elsevier Sci. Publ. Co., Amsterdam, NETH.

Davis, C. B., and A. G. Van der Valk. 1978. Litter decomposition in prairie glacial marshes. In Freshwater Wetlands. Ecological Processes and Management Potential, ed. R. E. Good, D. F. Whigham, and R. L. Simpson, pp. 99–113. Academic Press, New York.

Dubbe, D. R., E. G. Garver, and D. C. Pratt. 1988. Production of cattail (*Typha* spp.) biomass in Minnesota. Biomass 17: 17–104.

Ernsting, G., and F. B. Cross. 1987. Fishes of Cheyenne Bottoms and associated streams. In Cheyenne Bottoms. An Environmental Assessment. Kans. Biol. Survey and Kans. Geol. Survey, Lawrence, pp. 363–99.

Gates, D. M. 1971. The flow of energy in the biosphere. Sci. American 224(3): 88–100.

Griffith, M., and G. Welker. 1987. Invertebrates. In Cheyenne Bottoms. An Environmental Assessment. Kans. Biol. Survey and Kans. Geol. Survey, Lawrence, pp. 317–62.

Grodhaus, G. 1980. Aestivating Chironomid larvae associated with vernal pools. In Chironomidae, ed. D. A. Murray, pp. 315–22. Pergamon Press, Oxford, ENG.

Hilsenhoff, W. L. 1966. The biology of *Chironomus plumosus* (Diptera: Chironomidae) in Lake Winnebago, Wisconsin. Ann. Ent. Soc. Amer. 59: 465–73.

Hoffman, W. 1987a. The birds of Cheyenne Bottoms. In Cheyenne Bottoms. An Environmental Assessment. Kans. Biol. Survey and Kans. Geol. Survey, Lawrence, pp. 433–550.

———. 1987b. An ecological overview of the Cheyenne Bottoms marsh. In Cheyenne Bottoms. An Environmental Assessment. Kans. Biol. Survey and Kans. Geol. Survey, Lawrence, pp. 569–84.

Hoffman, W., and P. Arbetan. 1987. The mammals of Cheyenne Bottoms. In Cheyenne Bottoms. An Environmental Assessment. Kans. Biol. Survey and Kans. Geol. Survey, Lawrence, pp. 551–68.

Irwin, K. J., and J. T. Collins. 1987. Amphibians and reptiles of Cheyenne Bottoms. In Cheyenne Bottoms. An Environmental Assessment. Kans. Biol. Survey and Kans. Geol. Survey, Lawrence, pp. 401–32.

Klopatek, J. M. 1978. Nutrient dynamics of freshwater riverine marshes and the role of emergent macrophytes. In Freshwater Wetlands. Ecological Processes and Management Potential, ed. R. E. Good, D. F. Wigham, and R. L. Simpson, pp. 195–216. Academic Press, New York.

Kormondy, E. J. 1969. Concepts of Ecology. Prentice-Hall, Inc., Englewood Cliffs, NJ.

Mitsch, W. J., and J. G. Gosselink. 1986. Wetlands. Van Nostrand Reinhold Co., New York.

Oliver, D. R. 1971. Life history of the Chironomidae. Ann. Rev. Entomol. 16: 211–30.

Parmelee, D. F., M. D. Schwilling, and H. A. Stephens. 1969. Charadriiform birds of Cheyenne Bottoms. Part I. Kans. Ornithol. Soc. Bull. 20: 9–13; Part II. Kans. Ornithol. Soc. Bull. 20: 17–24.

Van der Valk, A. G., and C. B. Davis. 1978. Primary production in prairie glacial marshes. In Freshwater Wetlands. Ecological Processes and Management Potential, ed. R. E. Good, D. F. Whigham, and R. L. Simpson, pp. 21–38. Academic Press, New York.

Weller, M. W., and L. H. Fredrickson. 1973. Avian ecology of a managed glacial marsh. Living Bird 12: 269–91.

5 ECOLOGICAL COMMUNITIES

Bishop, B. C. 1976. Landsat looks at hometown Earth. National Geographic 150 (1): 140–47.

Brooks, R. E., and C. Kuhn. 1987. The vegetation of Cheyenne Bottoms. In Cheyenne Bottoms. An Environmental Assessment. Kans. Biol. Survey and Kans. Geol. Survey, Lawrence, pp. 251–315.

Ernsting, G. W. 1984. Nesting distribution in Kansas of selected colonial nesting herons in 1982 and 1983. Master's thesis, Fort Hays State Univ., Hays, KS.

Ernsting, G. W., and F. B. Cross. 1987. Fishes of Cheyenne Bottoms and associated streams. In Cheyenne Bottoms. An Environmental Assessment. Kans. Biol. Survey and Kans. Geol. Survey, Lawrence, pp. 363–99.

Griffith, M., and G. Welker. Invertebrates. In Cheyenne Bottoms. An Environmental Assessment. Kans. Biol. Survey and Kans. Geol. Survey, Lawrence, pp. 317–62.

Hoffman, W. 1987. The birds of Cheyenne Bottoms. In Cheyenne Bottoms. An Environmental Assessment. Kans. Biol. Survey and Kans. Geol. Survey, Lawrence, pp. 433–550.

Hoffman, W., and P. Arbetan. 1987. The mammals of Cheyenne Bottoms. In Cheyenne Bottoms. An Environmental Assessment. Kans. Biol. Survey and Kans. Geol. Survey, Lawrence, pp. 551–68.

Irwin, K. J., and J. T. Collins. 1987. Amphibians and reptiles of Cheyenne Bottoms. In Cheyenne Bottoms. An Environmental Assessment. Kans. Biol. Survey and Kans. Geol. Survey, Lawrence, pp. 401–32.

Orians, G. H. 1985. Blackbirds of the Americas. Univ. Washington Press, Seattle.

Parmelee, D. F. 1963. Notes on the Phalaropodidae of Cheyenne Bottoms. Kans. Ornithol. Soc. Bull. 14: 12.

Parmelee, D. F., M. D. Schwilling, and H. A. Stephens. 1970. Gruiform birds of Cheyenne Bottoms. Kans Ornithol. Soc. Bull. 21: 25–27.

Rice, O. O. 1956. The avocet on Cheyenne Bottoms. Kans. Ornithol. Soc. Bull. 7: 11–12.

Schwilling, M. D. 1971a. Bobolinks nest again in Kansas. Kans. Ornithol. Soc. Bull. 22: 14–15.

———. 1971b. Rapid increase and dispersal of boat-tailed grackles in Kansas. Kans. Ornithol. Soc. Bull. 22: 15–16.

———. 1975. Louisiana heron nest in Barton County, Kans. Ornithol. Soc. Bull. 26: 22.

Thompson, M. C., and C. Ely. 1989. Birds in Kansas. Univ. Kansas Mus. Nat. Hist., Public Educ. Ser. No. 11, vol. 1: xv, 1–404.

Weller, M. W. 1987. Freshwater Marshes. Ecology and Management. 2d ed. Univ. Minnesota Press, Minneapolis.

Zuvanich, J. R. 1963a. Forster terns breeding in Kansas. Kans. Ornithol. Soc. Bull. 14: 1–3.

———. 1963b. White-faced ibis nesting at Cheyenne Bottoms. Kans. Ornithol. Soc. Bull. 14: 11.

6 SHOREBIRD PATTERNS OF PASSAGE

American Ornithologists' Union. 1983. Check-list of North American Birds, 6th ed. Amer. Ornithol. Union, Allen Press, Lawrence, KS.

Evans, P. R., and M. W. Pienkowski. 1984. Population dynamics of shorebirds. Behav. Marine Animals 5: 83–123.

Hall, H. M. 1960. A Gathering of Shore Birds. Devin-Adair Co.,

New York.

Harrington, B. A., and R. I. G. Morrison. 1979. Semipalmated sandpiper migration in North America. In Shorebirds in Marine Environments, ed. F. A. Pitelka, Studies in Avian Biol. 2: 83–100. Cooper Ornithol. Soc., Allen Press, Lawrence, KS.

Jehl, J. R., Jr. 1979. The autumnal migration of Baird's sandpiper. In Shorebirds in Marine Environments, ed. F. A. Pitelka, Studies in Avian Biol. 2: 55–68. Cooper Ornithol. Soc., Allen Press, Lawrence, KS.

Matthiessen, P. 1973. The Wind Birds. Viking Press, New York.

Morrison, R. I. G. 1984. Migration systems of some New World shorebirds. Behav. Marine Animals 6: 125–202.

Parmelee, D. F., M. D. Schwilling, and H. A. Stephens. 1969. Charadriiform birds of Cheyenne Bottoms. Part I. Kans. Ornithol. Soc. Bull. 20: 9–13. Part II. Kans. Ornithol. Soc. Bull. 20: 17–24.

Sauer, E. G. F. 1963. Migration habits of golden plovers. Proc. XIII Internat. Ornithol. Congr.: 454–67.

Senner, S. E., and E. F. Martinez. 1982. A review of western sandpiper migration in interior North America. Southwestern Nat. 27: 149–59.

Snyder, L. L. 1957. Arctic Birds of Canada. Univ. Toronto Press, Toronto.

Welty, J. C., and L. Baptista. 1988. The Life of Birds. 4th ed. Saunders College Publishing, New York.

7 THE PROBLEM

Anonymous. 1972. Great Bend, Kansas. A Historical Portrait of the City. Centennial Book Committee, Great Bend.

Bagley, J. O. 1989. Availability of water in Walnut Creek, its tributaries, their valley alluviums, and hydraulically connected aquifers. Div. Water Res., Rept. 89–1. Kansas State Board of Agric., Topeka.

Bolin, B., J. Jäger, and B. R. Döös. 1986. The greenhouse effect, climatic change, and ecosystems. A synthesis of present knowledge. In SCOPE 29, The Greenhouse Effect, Climatic Change, and Ecosystems, ed. B. Bolin, B. D. Döös, J. Jäger, and R. A. Warrick, pp. 1–32. John Wiley & Sons, Chichester, West Sussex, ENG.

Graedel, T. E., and P. J. Crutzen. 1989. The changing atmosphere. Sci. American 261 (3): 58–68.

Kerr, R. A. 1989. The global warming is real. Science 243: 603.

Layher, W. G. 1989. Analysis of the biological assessment, Wet Walnut Creek subwatersheds nos. 1, 2, 3, and 5, prepared by the USDA Soil Conserv. Service. Environmental Services Sec., KDWP.

Lovejoy, T. E. 1988. Will unexpectedly the top blow off? BioScience 38: 722–26.

Miller, M. 1988. The way it was. Kansas Wildlife & Parks 45(4): 32–35.

Parr, D. 1987. Engineering assessment. An Environmental Assessment. Kans. Biol. Survey and Kans. Geol. Survey, Lawrence, pp. 617–21.

Roberts, L. 1988. Is there life after climatic change? Science 242: 1010–12.

———. 1989. How fast can trees migrate? Science 243: 735–37.

Schneider, S. H. 1989*a*. The greenhouse effect: Science and policy. Science 243: 771–81.

———. 1989*b*. The changing climate. Sci. American 261 (3): 70–79.

Schwilling, M. 1985. Cheyenne Bottoms. Kans. School Naturalist 32(2): 3–15.

Tangley, L. 1988*a*. Preparing for climatic change. BioScience 38: 14–18.

———. 1988*b*. Greenhouse effect already here? Scientists call for action. BioScience 38: 538.

Welker, G. 1987. The effect of land use on runoff in the Cheyenne Bottoms watershed. An Environmental Assessment. Kans. Biol. Survey and Kans. Geol. Survey, Lawrence, pp. 121–48.

8 THE IMPORTANCE

Harrington, B. A. 1984. Arctic Shorebird Migration. Prelim. Rept. for Richard King Mellon Foundation, Pittsburgh, PA.

Layher, B., and L. Zuckerman. 1988. Water: the life blood of

Cheyenne Bottoms. Wildlife and Parks 45 (4): 40–41.

Lincoln, F. C. 1933. Banding of wild fowl furnishes data for the sportsman of this continent. Kansas. Maryland Conservationist, Summer: 22.

Martinez, E. F. 1979. Shorebird banding at the Cheyenne Bottoms Waterfowl Management Area. Wader Study Group Bull. 25: 40–41.

Myers, J. P. 1983. Conservation of migrating shorebirds: staging areas, geographic bottlenecks, and regional movements. Am. Birds 37: 23–25.

Myers, J. P., R. I. G. Morrison, P. Z. Antas, B. A. Harrington, T. E. Lovejoy, M. Sallaberry, S. E. Senner, and A. Tarak. 1987. Conservation strategy for migratory species. Amer. Sci. 75: 19–26.

Redelfs, A. E. 1983. Wetlands Values and Losses in the United States. Master's thesis, Oklahoma State Univ., Stillwater.

Senner, S. E., and M. A. Howe. 1984. Conservation of nearctic shorebirds. Behav. Marine Animals 5: 379–421.

Sicilian, S., and C. Coleman. 1987. The economic impact of Cheyenne Bottoms on Kansas and Barton County. In Cheyenne Bottoms. An Environmental Assessment. Kans. Biol. Survey and Kans. Geol. Survey, Lawrence, pp. 585–615.

Weller, M. W. 1987. Freshwater Marshes. Ecology and Wildlife Management. 2d ed. Univ. Minnesota Press, Minneapolis.

Wentz, W. A. 1988. An introduction to Cheyenne Bottoms. Wildlife and Parks 45(4): 30.

9 REPRIEVE AND HOPE

Bronowski, J. 1966. The Identity of Man. The Natural History Press, Garden City, NY.

Brundtland, G. H. 1989. Global change and our common future. Environment 31 (5): 16–20, 40–43.

Clark, W. C. 1989. Managing planet Earth. Sci. American 261 (3): 47–54.

Fredrickson, L., W. Hoffman, D. G. Huggins, T. McClain, D. Parr, and L. Vogler. 1987. Options for improving facilities and management. In Cheyenne Bottoms. An Environmental Assessment. Kans. Biol. Survey and Kans. Geol. Survey, Lawrence, pp. 623–80.

Kromm, D. E., and S. E. White. 1986. Public preferences for recommendations made by the High Plains–Ogallala aquifer study. Social Sci. Quart. 67: 843–54.

Layher, W. G. 1989. Analysis of the biological assessment, Wet Walnut Creek subwatersheds nos. 1, 2, 3, and 5, prepared by the USDA Soil Conserv. Service. Environmental Services Sect., KDWP.

Lovejoy, T. E. 1988. Will unexpectedly the top blow off? BioScience 38: 722–26.

McKibben, B. 1989. Reflections. The end of nature. The New Yorker. 11 Sept. 1989: 47–105.

Majumder, S. K. 1971. The Drama of Man and Nature. Charles E. Merrill Publ. Co., Columbus, OH.

Ruckelshaus, W. D. 1989. Toward a sustainable world. Sci. American 261 (3): 166–75.

Appendixes

The Plant and Vertebrate Biota of Cheyenne Bottoms

Appendix A
Vascular Plants

List published in Brooks, R. E., and C. Kuhn. 1987. The vegetation of Cheyenne Bottoms. In Cheyenne Bottoms. An Environmental Assessment. Kansas Biol. Survey and Kansas Geol. Survey, Lawrence, pp. 251–315. Names based on Great Plains Flora Assoc. 1986. Flora of the Great Plains. T. M. Barkley (ed.). Univ. Press of Kansas, Lawrence.

SALVINIACEAE, WATER FERN FAMILY

Azolla mexicana Presl.   mosquito fern

CUPRESSACEAE, CYPRESS FAMILY

Juniperus virginiana L.   red cedar

RANUNCULACEAE, BUTTERCUP FAMILY

Anemone caroliniana Walt.   Carolina anemone

PAPAVERACEAE, POPPY FAMILY

Argemone polyanthemos (Fedde) G. Ownby   prickly poppy

ULMACEAE, ELM FAMILY

Celtis occidentalis L.   hackberry

CANNABACEAE, HEMP FAMILY

Cannabis sativa L.   hemp

NYCTAGINACEAE, FOUR-O'CLOCK FAMILY

Mirabilis linearis (Pursh) Heimerl.   narrowleaf four-o'clock
Mirabilis nyctaginea (Michx.) MacM.   wild four-o'clock

AIZOACEAE, FIG-MARIGOLD FAMILY

Sesuvium verrucosum Raf.   sea purslane

CACTACEAE, CACTUS FAMILY

Opuntia macrorhiza Engelm.   plains prickly pear

CHENOPODIACEAE, GOOSEFOOT FAMILY

Atriplex argentea Nutt.   silver-scale saltbush
Atriplex subspicata (Nutt.) Rydb.   spearscale
Chenopodium berlandieri Moq.   pitseed goosefoot
Chenopodium dessicatum A. Nels.   desert goosefoot
Chenopodium glaucum L.   oak-leaved goosefoot
Chenopodium missouriense Aellen   Missouri goosefoot
Chenopodium pratericola Rydb.
Chenopodium rubrum L.   alkali blite
Cycloloma atriplicifolium (Spreng.) Coult.   winged pigweed
Kochia scoparia (L.) Schrad.   kochia
Salsola collina Pall.   tumbleweed
Salsola iberica Senn. & Pau   Russian thistle
Suaeda depressa (Pursh) S. Wats.   sea blite

AMARANTHACEAE, PIGWEED FAMILY

Amaranthus albus L.   tumbleweed
Amaranthus arenicola I. M. Johnst.   sandhills pigweed
Amaranthus graecizans L.   prostrate pigweed
Amaranthus hybridus L.   slender pigweed
Amaranthus retroflexus L.   rough pigweed
Amaranthus rudis Sauer   water-hemp

PORTULACACEAE, PURSLANE FAMILY

Portulaca oleracea L.   common purslane

MOLLUGINACEAE, CARPETWEED FAMILY

Mollugo verticillata L.   carpetweed

POLYGONACEAE, BUCKWHEAT FAMILY

Polygonum arenastrum Jord.   knotweed
Polygonum ramosissimum Michx.   knotweed
Polygonum amphibium L.   water smartweed
Polygonum bicorne Raf.   pink smartweed
Polygonum hydropiper L.   water pepper
Polygonum lapathifolium L.   pale smartweed
Polygonum pensylvanicum L.   Pennsylvania smartweed
Rumex altissimus Wood   pale dock
Rumex crispus L.   curly dock
Rumex stenophyllus Ledeb.   narrow-leaved dock

MALVACEAE, MALLOW FAMILY

Abutilon theophrasti Medic.   velvet-leaf
Callirhoe involucrata (T. & G.) A. Gray   purple poppy mallow

TAMARICACEAE, TAMARISK FAMILY

Tamarix ramosissima Ledeb.   salt cedar

CUCURBITACEAE, GOURD FAMILY

Cucurbita foetidissima H. B. K.   buffalo-gourd

SALICACEAE, WILLOW FAMILY

Populus deltoides Marsh.   cottonwood
Salix exigua Nutt.   sandbar willow
Salix nigra Marsh.   black willow

CAPPARACEAE, CAPER FAMILY

Polanisia dodecandra (L.) DC.   clammy-weed

BRASSICACEAE, MUSTARD FAMILY

Capsella bursa-pastoris (L.) Medic.   shepherd's purse
Descurainia pinnata (Walt.) Britt.   tansy mustard
Descurainia sophia (L.) Webb   flixweed
Erysimum repandum L.   bushy wallflower
Lepidium densiflorum Schrad.   peppergrass
Lepidium oblongum Small   peppergrass
Rorippa palustris (L.) Bess.   bog yellow cress
Rorippa sinuata (Nutt.) Hitchc.   spreading yellow cress
Thlaspi arvense L.   pennycress

ROSACEAE, ROSE FAMILY

Prunus virginiana L.   choke cherry
Rosa arkansana Porter   prairie wild rose

MIMOSACEAE, MIMOSA FAMILY

Desmanthus illinoensis (Michx.) MacM.   Illinois bundleflower
Desmanthus leptolobus T. & G.   slender-lobed bundleflower

FABACEAE, LEGUME FAMILY

Amorpha canescens Pursh   lead plant
Amorpha fruticosa L.   false indigo
Astragalus lotiflorus Hook.   lotus milk-vetch
Astragalus missouriensis Nutt.   Missouri milk-vetch
Astragalus mollissimus Torr.   woolly locoweed
Glycyrrhiza lepidota Pursh   wild licorice

169

Medicago sativa L.   alfalfa
Melilotus alba Medic.   white sweet clover
Melilotus officinalis (L.) Pall.   yellow sweet clover
Vicia americana Muhl. ex Willd.   American vetch

ELAEAGNACEAE, RUSSIAN OLIVE FAMILY

Elaeagnus angustifolia L.   Russian olive

LYTHRACEAE, LOOSESTRIFE FAMILY

Ammannia coccinea Rottb.
Ammannia robusta Herr. & Regal   purple ammannia
Lythrum californicum T. & G.   California loosestrife

ONAGRACEAE, PRIMROSE FAMILY

Gaura parviflora Dougl.   velvety gaura
Oenothera laciniata Hill   cut-leaved evening primrose
Oenothera villosa Thunb.   common evening primrose

EUPHORBIACEAE, SPURGE FAMILY

Croton texensis (Kl.) Muell. Arg.   Texas croton
Euphorbia dentata Michx.   toothed spurge
Euphorbia glyptosperma Engelm.   ridge-seeded spurge
Euphorbia hexagona Nutt.   six-angled spurge
Euphorbia maculata L.   spotted spurge
Euphorbia marginata Pursh   snow-on-the-mountain
Euphorbia prostrata Ait.
Euphorbia serpens H. B. K.   round-leaved spurge
Euphorbia spathulata Lam.
Euphorbia stictospora Engelm.   mat spurge

VITACEAE, GRAPE FAMILY

Vitis riparia Michx.   river-bank grape

LINACEAE, FLAX FAMILY

Linum rigidum Pursh   compact stiffstem flax

ACERACEAE, MAPLE FAMILY

Acer negundo L.   box elder

ZYGOPHYLLACEAE, CALTROP FAMILY

Tribulus terrestris L.   puncture vine

OXALIDACEAE, WOOD SORREL FAMILY

Oxalis dillenii Jacq.   gray-green wood sorrel

APIACEAE, PARSLEY FAMILY

Conium maculatum L.   poison hemlock
Daucus carota L.   wild carrot

APOCYNACEAE, DOGBANE FAMILY

Apocynum cannabinum L.   hemp dogbane

ASCLEPIADACEAE, MILKWEED FAMILY

Asclepias latifolia (Torr.) Raf.   broadleaf milkweed
Asclepias speciosa Torr.   showy milkweed
Asclepias sullivantii Engelm.   smooth milkweed
Asclepias syriaca L.   common milkweed
Asclepias verticillata L.   whorled milkweed
Asclepias viridis Walt.   spider milkweed

SOLANACEAE, NIGHTSHADE FAMILY

Datura innoxia P. Mill   sacred datura, Indian apple
Physalis longifolia Nutt.   common ground cherry
Physalis pumila Nutt.   prairie ground cherry
Solanum elaeagnifolium Cav.   silver-leaf nightshade
Solanum interius Rydb.   plains black nightshade
Solanum rostratum Dun.   buffalo bur

CONVOLVULACEAE, MORNING GLORY FAMILY

Calystegia macounii (Greene) Brummitt   hedge bindweed
Convolvulus arvensis L.   field bindweed

CUSCUTACEAE, DODDER FAMILY

Cuscuta indecora Choisy   large alfalfa dodder

BORAGINACEAE, BORAGE FAMILY

Heliotropium curassavicum L.   wild heliotrope

VERBENACEAE, VERVAIN FAMILY

Lippia cuneifolia (Torr.) Steud.   wedgeleaf fog-fruit
Lippia lanceolata (Michx.) Greene   northern fog-fruit
Lippia nodiflora (L.) Michx.
Verbena bipinnatifida Nutt.   Dakota verbena
Verbena bracteata Lag. & Rodr.   prostrate verbena
Verbena stricta Vent.   hoary verbena

PLANTAGINACEAE, PLANTAIN FAMILY

Plantago elongata Pursh   slender plantain

OLEACEAE, OLIVE FAMILY
Fraxinus pennsylvanica Marsh.   green ash

SCROPHULARIACEAE, FIGWORT FAMILY

Bacopa rotundifolia (Michx.) Wettst.   disk water-hyssop
Linaria vulgaris Hill   butter-and-eggs
Veronica peregrina L.   purslane speedwell

PEDALIACEAE, PEDALIUM FAMILY

Proboscidea louisianica (P. Mill.) Thell.   devil's claw

LENTIBULARIACEAE, BLADDERWORT FAMILY

Utricularia vulgaris L.   common bladderwort

RUBIACEAE, MADDER FAMILY

Cephalanthus occidentalis L.   common buttonbush
Galium aparine L.   catchweed bedstraw

ASTERACEAE, SUNFLOWER FAMILY

Achillea millefolium L.   yarrow
Ambrosia psilostachya DC.   western ragweed
Ambrosia trifida L.   giant ragweed
Artemesia ludoviciana Nutt.   white sage
Aster ericoides L.   heath aster
Aster simplex Willd.   panicled aster
Aster subulatus Michx.   shinners, annual saltmarsh aster
Baccharis salicina T. & G.   willow baccharis
Bidens comosa (A. Gray) Wieg.   leafybract beggar-tick
Bidens frondosa L.   beggar-tick
Cirsium undulatum (Nutt.) Spreng.   wavy-leaf thistle
Cirsium vulgare (Savi.) Ten.   bull thistle
Conyza canadensis (L.) Cronq.   horseweed
Coreopsis tinctoria Nutt.   plains coreopsis
Erechtites hieracifolia (L.) Raf. ex DC.   American burnweed
Erigeron strigosus Muhl. ex Willd.   daisy fleabane
Grindelia squarrosa (Pursh) Dunal   curlycup gumweed
Haplopappus ciliatus (Nutt.)   goldenweed
Helianthus annuus L.   common sunflower
Helianthus ciliaris DC.   Texas blueweed
Helianthus petiolaris Nutt.   plains sunflower
Heterotheca latifolia Buckl.   camphorweed
Iva annua L.   annual sumpweed, marsh elder
Kuhnia eupatorioides L.   false boneset
Lactuca canadensis L.   wild lettuce

Lactuca ludoviciana (Nutt.) Ridd.   western wild lettuce
Lactuca serriola L.   prickly lettuce
Pluchea odorata (L.) Cass.   camphorweed
Pyrrhopappus grandiflorus (Nutt.) Nutt.   tuber false dandelion
Ratibida columnifera (Nutt.) Woot. & Standl.   prairie coneflower
Solidago canadensis L.   Canada goldenrod
Sonchus asper (L.) Hill   sow thistle
Taraxacum officinale Weber   dandelion
Thelesperma megapotamicum (Spreng.) O. Ktze.   slender greenthread
Tragopogon dubius Scop.   western salsify
Vernonia fasciculata Michx.   western ironweed
Xanthium strumarium L.   cocklebur

ALISMATACEAE, WATER PLANTAIN FAMILY

Echinodorus rostratus (Nutt.) Engelm.   erect burhead

JUNCAGINACEAE, ARROWGRASS FAMILY

Triglochin martima L.   arrowgrass

NAJADACEAE, NAIAD FAMILY

Najas guadalupensis (Spreng.)   southern naiad

LEMNACEAE, DUCKWEED FAMILY

Lemna minor L.   common duckweed
Spirodela polyrrhiza (L.) Schleid.   greater duckweed

COMMELINACEAE, SPIDERWORT FAMILY

Tradescantia bracteata Small   bracted spiderwort

JUNCACEAE, RUSH FAMILY

Juncus interior Wieg.   inland rush
Juncus torreyi Cov.   Torrey's rush

CYPERACEAE, SEDGE FAMILY

Carex brevior (Dewey) Mack.   straw sedge
Carex gravida Bailey
Carex laeviconica Dewey   smoothcone sedge
Cyperus acuminatus T. & H.   tapeleaf sedge
Cyperus lupulinus (Spreng.)   Marcks
Cyperus odoratus L.   slender flatsedge
Eleocharis acicularis (L.) R. & S.   needle spikesedge
Eleocharis obtusa (Willd.) Schult.   blunt spikesedge
Eleocharis parvula (R. & S.) Link ex Buff. & Fingerbr.
Eleocharis xyridiformis Fern. & Brack.   spikesedge

Scirpus acutus Muhl.   bulrush
Scirpus fluviatilis (Torr.) A. Gray   river bulrush
Scirpus heterochaetus Chase   slender bulrush
Scirpus maritimus L.   alkali bulrush
Scirpus pungens Vahl   American bulrush

POACEAE, GRASS FAMILY

Agropyron cristatum (L.) Gaertn.   crested wheatgrass
Agropyron elongatum (Host.) Beauv.   tall wheatgrass
Agropyron smithii Rydb.   western wheatgrass
Agrostis hyemalis (Walt.) B.S.P.   ticklegrass
Alopecurus carolinianus Walt.   Carolina foxtail
Andropogon bladhii Retz.   Caucasian bluestem
Andropogon gerardii Vit.   big bluestem
Andropogon hallii Hack.   sand bluestem
Andropogon saccharoides Sw.   silver bluestem
Andropogon scoparius Michx.   little bluestem
Aristida longispica Poir.   slimspike three-awn
Aristida oligantha Michx.   prairie three-awn
Bouteloua curtipendula (Michx.) Torr.   sideoats grama
Bouteloua gracilis (H.B.K.) Lag. ex Griffiths   blue grama
Bromus inermis Leyss.   smooth brome
Bromus japonicus Thunb.   Japanese brome
Bromus tectorum L.   downy brome
Buchloë dactyloides (Nutt.) Engelm.   buffalo grass
Cenchrus longispinus (Hack.) Fern.   sandbur
Chloris verticillata Nutt.   windmill grass
Cinna arundinacea L.   woodreed
Cynodon dactylon (L.) Pers.   Bermuda grass
Digitaria ischaemum (Schreb. ex Schweigg.) Schreb ex Muhl.   smooth
    crabgrass
Digitaria sanguinalis (L.) Scop.   hairy crabgrass
Distichlis spicata (L.) Greene   inland saltgrass
Echinochloa crusgalli (L.) Beauv.   barnyard grass
Echinochloa crus-pavonis (H.B.K.)   Schult.
Echinochloa muricata (Beauv.) Fern.   barnyard grass
Elymus canadensis L.   Canada wild rye
Elymus virginicus L.   Virginia wild rye
Eragrostis cilianensis (All.) E. Mosher   stinkgrass
Eragrostis pectinacea (Michx.) Nees   Carolina lovegrass
Eragrostis reptans (Michx.) Nees   creeping lovegrass
Eragrostis spectabilis (Pursh) Steud.   purple lovegrass
Eriochloa contracta Hitchc.   prairie cupgrass
Festuca arundinacea Schreb.   tall fescue

Hordeum jubatum L.   foxtail barley
Hordeum pusillum Nutt.   little barley
Leptochloa fascicularis (Lam.) A. Gray   bearded sprangletop
Leptoloma cognatum (Schult.) Chase   fall witchgrass
Muhlenbergia asperifolia (Nees & Mey.) Parodi   scratchgrass
Panicum capillare L.   common witchgrass
Panicum dichotomiflorum Michx.   fall panicum
Panicum hillmanii Chase   Hillman's witchgrass
Panicum virgatum L.   switchgrass
Paspalum setaceum Michx.   sand paspalum
Phalaris arundinacea L.   reed canary grass
Poa arida Vasey   plains bluegrass
Polypogon monspeliensis (L.) Desf.   rabbitfoot grass
Schedonnardus paniculatus (Nutt.) Trel.   tumblegrass
Setaria geniculata (Lam.) Beauv.   knotroot bristlegrass
Setaria glauca (L.) Beauv.   yellow foxtail
Setaria viridis (L.) Beauv.   green foxtail
Sitanion hystrix (Nutt.) J.G.Sm.   squirreltail
Sorghum halepense (L.) Pers.   Johnson-grass
Spartina pectinata Link   prairie cordgrass
Sphenopholis obtusata (Michx.) Scribn.   wedgegrass
Sporobolus airoides (Torr.) Torr.   alkali sacaton
Sporobolus asper (Michx.) Kunth   rough dropseed
Sporobolus cryptandrus (Torr.) A. Gray   sand dropseed
Sporobolus neglectus Nash   poverty grass

SPARGANIACEAE, BUR-REED FAMILY

Sparganium eurycarpum Engelm.   giant bur-reed

TYPHACEAE, CATTAIL FAMILY

Typha angustifolia L.   narrow-leaved cattail
Typha latifolia L.   broad-leaved cattail

PONTEDERIACEAE, PICKERELWEED FAMILY

Heteranthera limosa (Sw.) Willd.   blue mud plantain

LILIACEAE, LILY FAMILY

Allium perdulce S. V. Fraser
Smilacina stellata (L.) Desf.   false Solomon's seal, spikenard

Appendix B
Fish

List published in Ernsting, G. W., and F. B. Cross. 1987. Fishes of Cheyenne Bottoms and associated streams. In Cheyenne Bottoms. An Environmental Assessment. Kansas Biol. Survey and Kansas Geol. Survey, Lawrence, pp. 363–99. Names based on Committee on Names of Fishes (C. R. Robins, Ch.). 1980. A List of Common and Scientific Names of Fishes from the United States and Canada. 4th ed., Amer. Fish. Soc. 5p. Publ. No. 12.

Common Carp   *Cyprinus carpio* Linnaeus
Red Shiner   *Notropis lutrensis* (Baird & Girard)
Sand Shiner   *Notropis stramineus* (Cope)
Fathead Minnow   *Pimephales promelas* (Rafinesque)
Black Bullhead   *Ictalurus melas* (Rafinesque)
Plains Killifish   *Fundulus zebrinus* Jordan & Gilbert
Largemouth Bass   *Micropterus salmoides* (Lacepede)
Green Sunfish   *Lepomis cyanellus* Rafinesque
Orangespotted Sunfish   *Lepomis humilis* (Girard)
White Crappie   *Pomoxis annularis* Rafinesque

Appendix C
Amphibians and Reptiles

List published in Irwin, K. J., and J. T. Collins. 1987. Amphibians and reptiles of Cheyenne Bottoms. In Cheyenne Bottoms. An Environmental Assessment. Kansas Biol. Survey and Kansas Geol. Survey, Lawrence, pp. 401–32. Names based on Collins, J. T. 1982. Amphibians and Reptiles in Kansas. 2d ed. Univ. Kansas Mus. Nat. Hist., Public Educ. Ser. No. 8, Lawrence.

Tiger Salamander   *Ambystoma tigrinum* (Green)
Plains Spadefoot   *Scaphiopus bombifrons* Cope
Great Plains Toad   *Bufo cognatus* Say
Woodhouse's Toad   *Bufo woodhousei* (Girard)
Cricket Frog   *Acris crepitans blanchardi* Harper
Spotted Chorus Frog   *Pseudacris clarki* Fitzinger
Western Chorus Frog   *Pseudacris triseriata* Wied
Plains Leopard Frog   *Rana blairi* Mecham, Littlejohn, Oldham,
    Brown and Brown
Bullfrog   *Rana catesbeiana* Shaw

Common Snapping Turtle   *Chelydra serpentina* (Linnaeus)
Yellow Mud Turtle   *Kinosternon flavescens* (Agassiz)
Painted Turtle   *Chrysemys picta belli* (Gray)
Slider   *Chrysemys scripta elegans* (Wied)
Spiny Softshell   *Trionyx spiniferus hartwegi* Conant & Goin

Great Plains Skink   *Eumeces obsoletus* (Baird & Girard)
Racerunner   *Cnemidophorus sexlineatus viridis* Lowe
Racer   *Coluber constrictor flaviventris* Say
Bullsnake   *Pituophis melanoleucus sayi* (Schlegel)
Prairie Kingsnake   *Lampropeltis calligaster* (Harlan)
Common Kingsnake   *Lampropeltis getulus* Stejneger
Plains Garter Snake   *Thamnophis radix haydeni* (Kennicott)

APPENDIX C: AMPHIBIANS AND REPTILES

Red-sided Garter Snake *Thamnophis sirtalis parietalis* (Say)
Lined Snake *Tropidoclonion lineatum* (Hallowell)
Graham's Crayfish Snake *Regina grahami* Baird & Girard
Diamondback Water Snake *Nerodia rhombifera* (Hallowell)
Northern Water Snake *Nerodia sipeodon* (Linnaeus)
Massasauga *Sistrurus catenatus* (Rafinesque)

Appendix D
Birds

List published in Hoffman, W. 1987. The birds of Cheyenne Bottoms. In Cheyenne Bottoms. An Environmental Assessment. Kansas Biol. Survey and Kansas Geol. Survey, Lawrence, pp. 433–550, with modifications. Names based on Amer. Ornithologists' Union. 1983. Checklist of North American Birds. 6th ed. and subsequent supplements.

Common Loon   *Gavia immer* (Brunnich)
Pied-billed Grebe   *Podilymbus podiceps* (Linnaeus)
Horned Grebe   *Podiceps auritus* (Linnaeus)
Eared Grebe   *Podiceps nigricollis* Brehm
Western Grebe   *Aechmophorus occidentalis* (Lawrence)
Clark's Grebe   *Aechmophorus clarkii* (Lawrence)
American White Pelican   *Pelecanus erythrorhynchos* Gmelin
Brown Pelican   *Pelecanus occidentalis* Linnaeus
Double-crested Cormorant   *Phalacrocorax auritus* (Lesson)
Olivaceous Cormorant   *Phalacrocorax olivaceus* (Humboldt)
Anhinga   *Anhinga anhinga* (Linnaeus)
American Bittern   *Botaurus lentiginosus* (Rackett)
Least Bittern   *Ixobrychus exilis* (Gmelin)
Great Blue Heron   *Ardea herodias* Linnaeus
Great Egret   *Casmerodius albus* (Linnaeus)
Snowy Egret   *Egretta thula* (Molina)
Little Blue Heron   *Egretta caerulea* (Linnaeus)
Tricolor Heron   *Egretta tricolor* (Müller)
Cattle Egret   *Bubulcus ibis* (Linnaeus)
Green-backed Heron   *Butroides striatus* (Linnaeus)
Black-crowned Night-heron   *Nycticorax nycticorax* (Linnaeus)
Yellow-crowned Night-heron   *Nyctanassa violaceus* (Linnaeus)
White Ibis   *Eudocimus albus* (Linnaeus)
White-faced Ibis   *Plegadis chihi* (Vieillot)
Roseate Spoonbill   *Ajaia ajaja* (Linnaeus)

Wood Stork   *Mycteria americana* Linnaeus
Fulvous Whistling-duck   *Denrocygna bicolor* (Vieillot)
Tundra Swan   *Cygnus columbianus* (Ord)
Greater White-fronted Goose   *Anser albifrons* (Scopoli)
Snow Goose   *Chen caerulescens* (Linnaeus)
Ross' Goose   *Chen rossii* (Cassin)
Brant   *Branta bernicla* (Linnaeus)
Canada Goose   *Branta canadensis* (Linnaeus)
Wood Duck   *Aix sponsa* (Linnaeus)
Green-winged Teal   *Anas crecca* Linnaeus
American Black Duck   *Anas rubripes* Brewster
Mottled Duck   *Anas fulvigula* Ridgway
Mallard   *Anas platyrhynchos* Linnaeus
Northern Pintail   *Anas acuta* Linnaeus
Blue-winged Teal   *Anas discors* Linnaeus
Cinnamon Teal   *Anas cyanoptera* Vieillot
Northern Shoveler   *Anas clypeata* Linnaeus
Gadwall   *Anas strepera* Linnaeus
Eurasian Wigeon   *Anas penelope* Linnaeus
American Wigeon   *Anas americana* Gmelin
Canvasback   *Aythya valisinaria* (Wilson)
Redhead   *Aythya americana* (Eyton)
Ring-necked Duck   *Aythya collaris* (Donovan)
Greater Scaup   *Aythya marila* (Linnaeus)
Lesser Scaup   *Aythya affinis* (Eyton)
Oldsquaw   *Clangula hyemalis* (Linnaeus)
Black Scoter   *Melanitta nigra* (Linnaeus)
Surf Scoter   *Melanitta perspicillata* (Linnaeus)
White-winged Scoter   *Melanitta fusca* (Linnaeus)
Common Goldeneye   *Bucephala clangula* (Linnaeus)
Bufflehead   *Bucephala albeola* (Linnaeus)
Hooded Merganser   *Lophodytes cucullatus* (Linnaeus)
Common Merganser   *Mergus merganser* Linnaeus
Red-breasted Merganser   *Mergus serrator* Linnaeus
Ruddy Duck   *Oxyura jamaicensis* (Gmelin)
Turkey Vulture   *Cathartes aura* (Linnaeus)
Osprey   *Pandion haliaetus* (Linnaeus)
Mississippi Kite   *Ictinia mississippiensis* (Wilson)
Bald Eagle   *Haliaeetus leucocephalus* (Linnaeus)
Northern Harrier   *Circus cyaneus* (Linnaeus)
Sharp-shinned Hawk   *Accipiter striatus* Vieillot
Cooper's Hawk   *Accipiter cooperii* (Bonaparte)
Harris' Hawk   *Parabuteo unicinctus* (Temminck)
Red-shouldered Hawk   *Buteo lineatus* (Gmelin)

Broad-winged Hawk   *Buteo brachyurus* Vieillot
Swainson's Hawk   *Buteo swainsoni* Bonaparte
Red-tailed Hawk   *Buteo jamaicensis* (Gmelin)
Ferruginous Hawk   *Buteo regalis* (Gray)
Rough-legged Hawk   *Buteo lagopus* (Pontoppidan)
Golden Eagle   *Aquila chrysaetos* (Linnaeus)
American Kestrel   *Falco sparverius* Linnaeus
Merlin   *Falco columbarius* Linnaeus
Peregrine Falcon   *Falco peregrinus* Tunstall
Gyrfalcon   *Falco rusticolus* Linnaeus
Prairie Falcon   *Falco mexicanus* Schlegel
Ring-necked Pheasant   *Phasianus colchicus* Linnaeus
Greater Prairie-chicken   *Tympanuchus cupido* (Linnaeus)
Wild Turkey   *Meleagris gallopavo* Linnaeus
Northern Bobwhite   *Colinus virginus* (Linnaeus)
Yellow Rail   *Coturnicops noveboracensis* (Gmelin)
Black Rail   *Laterallus jamaicensis* (Gmelin)
King Rail   *Rallus elegans* Audubon
Virginia Rail   *Rallus limicola* Vieillot
Sora   *Porzana carolina* (Linnaeus)
Common Moorhen   *Gallinula chloropus* (Linnaeus)
American Coot   *Fulica americana* Gmelin
Sandhill Crane   *Grus canadensis* (Linnaeus)
Whooping Crane   *Grus americana* (Linnaeus)
Black-bellied Plover   *Pluvialis squatarola* (Linnaeus)
Lesser Golden-plover   *Pluvialis dominica* (Müller)
Snowy Plover   *Charadrius alexandrinus* Linnaeus
Semipalmated Plover   *Charadrius semipalmatus* Bonaparte
Piping Plover   *Charadrius melodus* Ord
Killdeer   *Charadrius vociferus* Linnaeus
Mountain Plover   *Charadrius montanus* Townsend
Black-necked Stilt   *Himantopus mexicanus* (Müller)
American Avocet   *Recurvirostra americana* Gmelin
Greater Yellowlegs   *Tringa melanoleuca* (Gmelin)
Lesser Yellowlegs   *Tringa flavipes* (Gmelin)
Solitary Sandpiper   *Tringa solitaria* Wilson
Willet   *Cataptrophorus semipalmatus* (Gmelin)
Spotted Sandpiper   *Actitis macularia* (Linnaeus)
Upland Sandpiper   *Bartramia longicauda* (Bechstein)
Whimbrel   *Numenius phaeopus* (Linnaeus)
Long-billed Curlew   *Numenius americanus* Bechstein
Hudsonian Godwit   *Limosa haemastica* (Linnaeus)
Marbled Godwit   *Limosa fedoa* (Linnaeus)
Ruddy Turnstone   *Arenaria interpres* (Linnaeus)

Red Knot   *Calidris canutus* (Linnaeus)
Sanderling   *Calidris alba* (Pallas)
Semipalmated Sandpiper   *Calidris pusilla* (Linnaeus)
Western Sandpiper   *Calidris mauri* (Cabanis)
Least Sandpiper   *Calidris minutilla* (Vieillot)
White-rumped Sandpiper   *Calidris fuscicollis* (Vieillot)
Baird's Sandpiper   *Calidris bairdii* (Coues)
Pectoral Sandpiper   *Calidris melanotos* (Vieillot)
Dunlin   *Calidris alpina* (Linnaeus)
Curlew Sandpiper   *Calidris ferruginea* (Pontoppidan)
Stilt Sandpiper   *Calidris himantopus* (Bonaparte)
Buff-breasted Sandpiper   *Tryngites subruficollis* (Vieillot)
Ruff   *Philomachus pugnax* (Linnaeus)
Short-billed Dowitcher   *Limnodromus griseus* (Gmelin)
Long-billed Dowitcher   *Limnodromus scolopaceus* (Say)
Common Snipe   *Gallinago gallinago* (Linnaeus)
Wilson's Phalarope   *Phalaropus tricolor* (Vieillot)
Red-necked Phalarope   *Phalaropus lobatus* (Linnaeus)
Red Phalarope   *Phalaropus fulicaria* (Linnaeus)
Pomarine Jaeger   *Stercorarius pomarinus* (Temminck)
Parasitic Jaeger   *Stercorarius parasiticus* (Linnaeus)
Long-tailed Jaeger   *Stercorarius longicaudus* Vieillot
Laughing Gull   *Larus atricilla* Linnaeus
Franklin's Gull   *Larus pipixcan* Wagler
Little Gull   *Larus minutus* Pallas
Common Black-headed Gull   *Larus ridibundus* Linnaeus
Bonaparte's Gull   *Larus philadelphia* (Ord)
Ring-billed Gull   *Larus delawarensis* Ord
California Gull   *Larus californicus* Lawrence
Herring Gull   *Larus argentatus* Pontoppidan
Thayer's Gull   *Larus thayeri* Brooks
Glaucous Gull   *Larus hyperboreus* Gunnerus
Black-legged Kittiwake   *Rissa tridactyla* (Linnaeus)
Sabine's Gull   *Xema sabini* (Sabine)
Caspian Tern   *Sterna caspia* Pallas
Common Tern   *Sterna hirundo* Linnaeus
Forster's Tern   *Sterna forsteri* Nuttall
Least Tern   *Sterna antillarum* (Lesson)
Black Tern   *Chlidonias niger* (Linnaeus)
Black Skimmer   *Rynchops niger* Linnaeus
Rock Dove   *Columba livia* Gmelin
Mourning Dove   *Zenaida macroura* (Linnaeus)
Common Ground-dove   *Columbina passerina* (Linnaeus)
Monk Parakeet   *Myiopsitta monachus* (Boddaert)

Black-billed Cuckoo   *Coccyzus erythropthalmus* (Wilson)
Yellow-billed Cuckoo   *Coccyzus americanus* (Linnaeus)
Barn Owl   *Tyto alba* (Scopoli)
Eastern Screech-owl   *Otus asio* (Linnaeus)
Great Horned Owl   *Bubo virginianus* (Gmelin)
Snowy Owl   *Nyctea scandiaca* (Linnaeus)
Burrowing Owl   *Athene cunicularia* (Molina)
Barred Owl   *Strix varia* Barton
Long-eared Owl   *Asio otus* (Linnaeus)
Short-eared Owl   *Asio flammeus* (Pontoppidan)
Common Nighthawk   *Chordeiles minor* (Forster)
Common Poorwill   *Phalaenoptilus nuttallii* (Audubon)
Whip-poor-will   *Caprimulgus vociferus* Wilson
Chimney Swift   *Chaetura pelagica* (Linnaeus)
Ruby-throated Hummingbird   *Archilochus colubris* (Linnaeus)
Rufous Hummingbird   *Selasphorus rufus* (Gmelin)
Belted Kingfisher   *Ceryle alcyon* (Linnaeus)
Red-headed Woodpecker   *Melanerpes erythrocephalus* (Linnaeus)
Red-bellied Woodpecker   *Melanerpes carolinus* (Linnaeus)
Yellow-bellied Sapsucker   *Sphyrapicus varius* (Linnaeus)
Downy Woodpecker   *Picoides pubescens* (Linnaeus)
Hairy Woodpecker   *Picoides villosus* (Linnaeus)
Northern Flicker   *Colaptes auratus* (Linnaeus)
Olive-sided Flycatcher   *Contopus borealis* (Swainson)
Western Wood-pewee   *Contopus sordidulus* Sclater
Eastern Wood-pewee   *Contopus virens* (Linnaeus)
Least Flycatcher   *Empidonax minimus* (Baird and Baird)
Hammond's Flycatcher   *Empidonax hammondii* (Xantus de Vesey)
Eastern Phoebe   *Sayornis phoebe* (Latham)
Say's Phoebe   *Sayornis saya* (Bonaparte)
Ash-throated Flycatcher   *Myiarchus cinerascens* (Lawrence)
Great-crested Flycatcher   *Myiarchus crinitus* (Linnaeus)
Western Kingbird   *Tyrannus verticalis* Say
Eastern Kingbird   *Tyrannus tyrannus* (Linnaeus)
Scissor-tailed Flycatcher   *Tyrannus forficatus* (Gmelin)
Horned Lark   *Eremophila alpestris* (Linnaeus)
Purple Martin   *Progne subis* (Linnaeus)
Tree Swallow   *Tachycineta bicolor* (Vieillot)
Violet-green Swallow   *Tachycineta thalassina* (Swainson)
Northern Rough-winged Swallow   *Stelgidopteryx serripennis*
    (Audubon)
Bank Swallow   *Riparia riparia* (Linnaeus)
Cliff Swallow   *Hirundo pyrrhonota* Vieillot
Barn Swallow   *Hirundo rustica* Linnaeus

185

Blue Jay   *Cyanocitta cristata* (Linnaeus)
Scrub Jay   *Aphelocoma coerulescens* (Bosc)
Clark's Nutcracker   *Nucifraga columbiana* (Wilson)
Black-billed Magpie   *Pica pica* (Linnaeus)
American Crow   *Corvus brachyrhynchos* Brehm
Black-capped Chickadee   *Parus atricapillus* Linnaeus
Tufted Titmouse   *Parus bicolor* Linnaeus
Red-breasted Nuthatch   *Sitta canadensis* Linnaeus
White-breasted Nuthatch   *Sitta carolinensis* Latham
Brown Creeper   *Certhia americana* Bonaparte
Rock Wren   *Salpinctes obsoletus* (Say)
Carolina Wren   *Thryothorus ludovicianus* (Latham)
Bewick's Wren   *Thyomanes bewickii* (Audubon)
House Wren   *Troglodytes aedon* Vieillot
Winter Wren   *Troglodytes trogoldytes* (Linnaeus)
Sedge Wren   *Cistothorus platensis* (Latham)
Marsh Wren   *Cistothorus palustris* (Wilson)
Golden-crowned Kinglet   *Regulus satrapa* Linneaus
Ruby-crowned Kinglet   *Regulus calendula* (Linnaeus)
Blue-gray Gnatcatcher   *Polioptila caerulea* (Linnaeus)
Eastern Bluebird   *Sialia sialis* (Linnaeus)
Mountain Bluebird   *Sialia currucoides* (Bechstein)
Townsend's Solitaire   *Myadestes townsendi* (Audubon)
Veery   *Catharus fuscescens* (Stephens)
Gray-cheeked Thrush   *Catharus minimus* (Lafresnaye)
Swainson's Thrush   *Catharus ustulatus* (Nuttall)
Hermit Thrush   *Catharus guttatus* (Pallas)
Wood Thrush   *Hylocichla mustelina* (Gmelin)
American Robin   *Turdus migratorius* Linnaeus
Gray Catbird   *Dumetella carolinensis* (Linnaeus)
Northern Mockingbird   *Mimus polyglottos* (Linnaeus)
Sage Thrasher   *Oreoscoptes montanus* (Townsend)
Brown Thrasher   *Toxostoma rufum* (Linnaeus)
Water Pipit   *Anthus spinoletta* (Linnaeus)
Sprague's Pipit   *Anthus spragueii* (Audubon)
Bohemian Waxwing   *Bombycilla garrulus* (Linnaeus)
Cedar Waxwing   *Bombycilla cedrorum* Vieillot
Loggerhead Shrike   *Lanius ludovicianus* Linnaeus
European Starling   *Sturnus vulgaris* Linnaeus
White-eyed Vireo   *Vireo griseus* (Boddaert)
Bell's Vireo   *Vireo bellii* Audubon
Solitary Vireo   *Vireo solitarius* (Wilson)
Warbling Vireo   *Vireo gilvus* (Vieillot)
Philadelphia Vireo   *Vireo philadelphicus* (Cassin)

Red-eyed Vireo   *Vireo olivaceus* (Linnaeus)
Tennessee Warbler   *Vermivora peregrina* (Wilson)
Orange-crowned Warbler   *Vermivora celata* (Say)
Nashville Warbler   *Vermivora ruficapilla* (Wilson)
Yellow Warbler   *Dendroica petechia* (Linnaeus)
Chestnut-sided Warbler   *Dendroica pensylvanica* (Linnaeus)
Yellow-rumped Warbler   *Dendroica coronata* (Linnaeus)
Black-throated Gray Warbler   *Dendroica nigrescens* (Townsend)
Black-throated Green Warbler   *Dendroica virens* (Gmelin)
Palm Warbler   *Dendroica palmarum* (Gmelin)
Bay-breasted Warbler   *Dendroica castanea* (Wilson)
Blackpoll Warbler   *Dendroica striata* (Forster)
Cerulean Warbler   *Dendroica cerulea* (Wilson)
Black-and-white Warbler   *Mniotilla varia* (Linnaeus)
American Redstart   *Setophaga ruticilla* (Linnaeus)
Prothonotary Warbler   *Protonotaria citrea* (Boddaert)
Ovenbird   *Seiurus aurocapillus* (Linnaeus)
Northern Waterthrush   *Seiurus noveboracensis* (Gmelin)
Louisiana Waterthrush   *Seiurus motacilla* (Vieillot)
Mourning Warbler   *Oporornis philadelphia* (Wilson)
MacGillivray's Warbler   *Oporornis tolmiei* (Townsend)
Common Yellowthroat   *Geothlypis trichas* (Linnaeus)
Wilson's Warbler   *Wilsonia pusilla* (Wilson)
Canada Warbler   *Wilsonia canadensis* (Linnaeus)
Yellow-breasted Chat   *Icteria virens* (Linnaeus)
Summer Tanager   *Piranga rubra* (Linnaeus)
Scarlet Tanager   *Piranga olivacea* (Gmelin)
Northern Cardinal   *Cardinalis cardinalis* (Linnaeus)
Rose-breasted Grosbeak   *Pheucticus ludovicianus* (Linnaeus)
Black-headed Grosbeak   *Pheucticus melanocephalus* (Swainson)
Blue Grosbeak   *Guiraca caerulea* (Linnaeus)
Lazuli Bunting   *Passerina amoena* (Say)
Indigo Bunting   *Passerina cyanea* (Linnaeus)
Painted Bunting   *Passerina ciris* (Linnaeus)
Dickcissel   *Spiza americana* (Gmelin)
Rufous-sided Towhee   *Pipilo erythrophthalmus* (Linnaeus)
Cassin's Sparrow   *Aimophila cassinii* (Woodhouse)
American Tree Sparrow   *Spizella arborea* (Wilson)
Chipping Sparrow   *Spizella passerina* (Bechstein)
Clay-colored Sparrow   *Spizella pallida* (Swainson)
Field Sparrow   *Spizella pusilla* (Wilson)
Vesper Sparrow   *Pooecetes gramineus* (Gmelin)
Lark Sparrow   *Chondestes grammacus* (Say)
Lark Bunting   *Calamospiza melanocorys* Stejneger

Savannah Sparrow   *Passerculus sandwichensis* (Gmelin)
Baird's Sparrow   *Ammodramus bairdii* (Audubon)
Grasshopper Sparrow   *Ammodramus savannarum* (Gmelin)
Henslow's Sparrow   *Ammodramus henslowii* (Audubon)
Le Conte's Sparrow   *Ammodramus leconteii* (Audubon)
Sharp-tailed Sparrow   *Ammodramus caudacutus* (Gmelin)
Fox Sparrow   *Passerella iliaca* (Merrem)
Song Sparrow   *Melospiza melodia* (Wilson)
Lincoln's Sparrow   *Melospiza lincolnii* (Audubon)
Swamp Sparrow   *Melospiza georgiana* (Latham)
White-throated Sparrow   *Zonotrichia albicollis* (Gmelin)
White-crowned Sparrow   *Zonotrichia leucophyrs* (Forster)
Harris' Sparrow   *Zonotrichia querula* (Nuttall)
Dark-eyed Junco   *Junco hyemalis* (Linnaeus)
Lapland Longspur   *Calcarius lapponicus* (Linnaeus)
Chestnut-collared Longspur   *Calcarius ornatus* (Townsend)
Snow Bunting   *Plectrophenax nivalis* (Linnaeus)
Bobolink   *Dolichonyx oryzivorus* (Linnaeus)
Red-winged Blackbird   *Agelaius phoeniceus* (Linnaeus)
Eastern Meadowlark   *Sturnella magna* (Linnaeus)
Western Meadowlark   *Sturnella neglecta* Audubon
Yellow-headed Blackbird   *Xanthocephalus xanthocephalus* (Bonaparte)
Rusty Blackbird   *Euphagus carolinus* (Müller)
Brewer's Blackbird   *Euphagus cyanocephalus* (Wagler)
Great-tailed Grackle   *Quiscalus mexicanus* (Gmelin)
Common Grackle   *Quiscalus quiscula* (Linnaeus)
Brown-headed Cowbird   *Molothrus ater* (Boddaert)
Orchard Oriole   *Icterus spurius* (Linnaeus)
Northern Oriole   *Icterus galbula* (Linnaeus)
Cassin's Finch   *Carpodacus cassinii* Baird
House Finch   *Carpodacus mexicanus* (Müller)
Red Crossbill   *Loxia curvirostra* Linnaeus
Pine Siskin   *Carduelis pinus* (Wilson)
American Goldfinch   *Carduelis tristis* (Linnaeus)
Evening Grosbeak   *Coccothraustes vespertinus* (Cooper)
House Sparrow   *Passer domesticus* (Linnaeus)

Appendix E
Mammals

List based on Hoffman, W., and P. Arbetan. 1987. The mammals of Cheyenne Bottoms. In Cheyenne Bottoms. An Environmental Assessment. Kansas Biol. Survey and Kansas Geol. Survey, Lawrence, pp. 551–68. Names based on Bee, J. W., G. E. Glass, R. W. Hoffmann, and R. R. Patterson. 1981. Mammals in Kansas. Univ. Kansas Mus. Nat. Hist., Public Educ. Ser. No. 7, Lawrence.

Opossum *Didelphis virginiana* Kerr
Southern Short-tailed Shrew *Blarina carolinensis* (Bachman)
Eastern Cottontail *Sylvilagus floridanus* (J. A. Allen)
Black-tailed Jack Rabbit *Lepus californicus melanotis* Mearns
Mearns Thirteen-lined Ground Squirrel *Spermophilus tridecemlineatus* (Mitchill)
Black-tailed Prairie Dog *Cynomys ludovicianus* (Ord)
Fox Squirrel *Sciurus niger rufiventer* Geoffroy
Beaver *Castor canadensis missouriensis* Bailey
Deer Mouse *Peromyscus maniculatus* (Wagner)
Hispid Cotton Rat *Sigmodon hispidus texianus* (Audubon & Bachman)
Prairie Vole *Microtus ochrogaster* (Wagner)
Muskrat *Ondatra zibethicus cinnamominus* (Hollister)
Coyote *Canis latrans* Say
Raccoon *Procyon lotor hirtus* Nelson & Goldman
Mink *Mustela vison letifera* Hollister
Badger *Taxidea taxus* (Schreber)
Striped Skunk *Mephitis mephitis* (Schreber)
Bobcat *Lynx rufus* (Schreber)
Mule Deer *Odocoileus hemionus* (Rafinesque)
White-tailed Deer *Odocoileus virginianus* (Zimmermann)

Index